PROFESSIONAL BUILDERS SECRETS

HOW CUSTOM HOME BUILDERS CAN SIGN MORE CONTRACTS AT HIGHER MARGINS, WHILE DELIVERING A BETTER CLIENT EXPERIENCE

PROFESSIONAL BUILDERS SECRETS

HOW CUSTOM HOME BUILDERS CAN SIGN MORE
CONTRACTS AT HIGHER MARGINS, WHILE DELIVERING
A BETTER CLIENT EXPERIENCE

Russ Stephens & Sky Stephens

Published by Best Seller Publishing®, Pasadena, CA
Best Seller Publishing® is a registered trademark.
Printed in the United States of America.
ISBN: 9798537730842

This publication is designed to provide accurate and authoritative information with regard to the subject matter covered. It is sold with the understanding that the publisher is not engaged in rendering legal, accounting, or other professional advice. If legal advice or other expert assistance is required, the services of a competent professional should be sought. The opinions expressed by the authors in this book are not endorsed by Best Seller Publishing® and are the sole responsibility of the author rendering the opinion.

For more information, please write:
Best Seller Publishing®
253 N. San Gabriel Blvd, Unit B
Pasadena, CA 91107
or call 1 (626) 765-9750
Visit us online at: www.BestSellerPublishing.org

TABLE OF CONTENTS

FOREWORD

It was around 2012 when Russ, Sky, and I started working together on a copywriting project.

They'd actually been closely following my email series until then, and had purchased a book called *Cashflow Advertising*.

After some initial discussions, they hired me to write the email sequences they'd crafted for a Customer Relationship Management (CRM) system for builders—a bank of email templates that would sit within a strategic sequence that builders could use to nurture and progress the leads they were generating.

What impressed me about them both was not just their approach to marketing but also their systematic methodology towards business.

I had a sense they were going to go from strength to strength, and that's exactly what they've continued to do.

While they're at the top of their field in the area of marketing, and travel all over the world to stay up-to-date with the latest strategies and technology (we've bumped into each other at a number of marketing conferences over the years), it's their combination of skills and experience that really sets them apart.

The systems and processes. The discipline. Managing teams. Mindset. The understanding of the building industry.

These are what have made them leaders in residential construction.

I may not be a builder, but I want to assure you that everything in this book is going to help you grow your building company while maintaining your margins.

Over the years, I've seen Russ and Sky test and tweak all of the systems they've created for residential home builders.

They're like master chefs who aren't satisfied until they've got the recipe just right.

And they don't just follow the experts and gurus, they question them.

Russ recently presented to a group I run about how, after testing the approach used by one of the most famous digital marketing educators on the planet, he decided to zig while everyone else was zagging.

And by doing the exact opposite, he quadrupled sales from the same advertising spend.

One thing's for sure: he takes the idea of testing and measurement to the next level.

And that's where the real value is for you as a builder.

What they share isn't simple theory.

It's not rehashed content.

It's battle-tested and verified to actually work with a particular target market before it's handed across to you.

Yes, it's the equivalent of rocking up to a five-star restaurant and being served a delicious, mouth-watering meal, instead of having to work out what ingredients and utensils you need, drive down to the shops, buy the items, and then make the meal yourself.

As a professional copywriter, I've worked in over 127 different industries and seen firsthand the challenges each of them faces.

As a builder, you're probably like most business owners.

You're great at what you do, but you don't have time to be a master at marketing, systems, operations, team building, and so on.

Or to leave your profession for four years and get an MBA.

You've probably got a family to feed, projects to stay on top of, kids to run around to events, and a full life which is bursting at the seams.

And once your business begins to grow, it can even lead to overwhelm.

That's where Russ and Sky are such an asset, no matter whether your business is treading water or thriving.

They won't be telling you how to build a quality home or where to find the right framing materials. You already know that.

Instead, they'll show you how to grow your company, just as they have for many others with their combination of marketing and systems know-how in the construction industry.

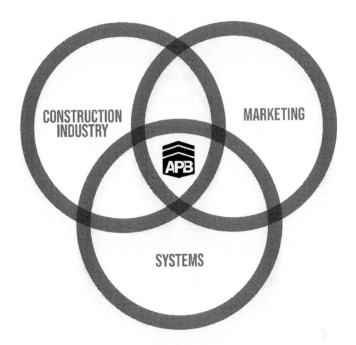

Figure I.I: The APB Difference

This is what truly sets them apart.

While wheels are important for a car, without an engine you're not going far. Likewise, when you have an engine and no wheels.

The reasons Russ and Sky are able to help building and construction companies thrive where so many other coaches fail are as follows (see *Figure I.I*):

First, they can get you leads with marketing.

Second, they help you set up systems to overcome the bottlenecks those leads create, so you can handle the demand and create the capacity to grow.

And finally, they understand your industry, via Russ's experience in operating a building company for five years and working with over four hundred builders within the Association of Professional Builders (APB) for over seven years.

Is there anyone else who has this amount of well-rounded experience, specifically focused on the building and construction industry?

Maybe there is, but I've yet to meet them.

After knowing and working with Russ and Sky for almost a decade now, I can assure you they are rock solid.

Their business has gone from strength to strength, and they have a rare combination of entrepreneurial zeal (full of ideas, innovation, and razor-sharp thinking) and solid business fundamentals that hundreds of builders have now leveraged to take their own companies to the next level.

You've got the resource to do the same with this eye-opening book. Now the ball's in your court.

Scott Bywater
Lead Generation Expert,
Direct Response Copywriter,
Email and Content Marketing Professional

INTRODUCTION

Back in 2011, I already understood that the whole sales process for a custom home builder was extraordinarily long and complex. I'd seen builders hemorrhaging profit in their contracts because of the additional items they were including for free after the contract had been signed. These items were either missed or forgotten about during the pricing process, or the clients were simply adding additional items post-contract and the builder felt obliged to keep them happy by not charging.

This is why my main business at the time was providing a service that would take care of all of the contract documentation for builders. So, instead of dealing with all the administration, builders could simply pay us to take the contract, prepare it, and then walk the client through every item step-by-step so that there was no confusion. This solution relieved custom home builders of a massive burden, and they were leaping at it.

The contract-preparation business also presented us with a unique opportunity for market research. Because we were independent, each time we prepared a contract and presented it to the builder's client, we would ask, "So why did you choose this builder over the others?" And because we were an unrelated party, they would tell us.

Now, the more I worked with builders, the more I realized that they were very price-focused. But custom home building is not a commodity, and therefore it should not be dependent on price. It really was a contradiction, and this contradiction carried over into the customers' responses.

What we discovered was that very rarely, in less than 20 percent of cases, did the consumer say that they chose a builder because they had the lowest price. In fact, 80 percent of the time the builder that the consumer had decided on wasn't the cheapest, but they had provided more documentation and more information, so the client felt comfortable that they were getting more value for their money. Meanwhile, at least 80 percent of builders told us they were losing jobs based on price.

There was a really big lie being told. And this was because consumers had discovered that lying about the price they'd been quoted was the quickest and easiest way to get rid of a builder. It was a lot easier than saying, "We didn't go with you because your documentation wasn't up to scratch." What's the benefit of saying that to a builder? They're only going to argue. "Well, tell me what you want, I'll put it in there!"

But if a consumer tells a builder, "I signed with someone else because they were $30,000 cheaper," What can the builder do? The customer has already signed the contract. So, when a consumer tells you they've gone with another builder because the price was lower, there's an 80 percent chance that what really happened was that they went with someone who had enough documentation to demonstrate the value of what they were offering and had made the customer feel comfortable.

This discovery was huge. And it formed the basis of the Association of Professional Builders (APB), because we knew the truth. While 80 percent of builders were saying, "I'm losing jobs on price," 80 percent of consumers were saying, "I went with this builder because they provided more documentation." When we knew that there was this disconnect, we set about building the systems that would enable professional builders to use the situation to their own advantage.

FROM COCONSTRUCT TO ACRIS TO THE APB

Another discovery I'd made with the contract-signing business was that communication was a problem on both sides. Whether it was a consumer talking about a builder or a builder talking about a consumer, most problems came down to communication. So that was the gap and the opportunity. It was why I started trying to create a system that would record on a timeline, in a systematic way, everything about the job as it progressed through the design stage and the preliminary stage.

So, one Saturday afternoon in 2011, as I was sitting in the back garden, enjoying the spring sunshine, my mobile phone rang. It was a Sydney builder who'd been getting my emails and was curious about the system I was creating to manage the sales process for custom home building companies. My goal was to create a seamless system that would keep track of all the items discussed during the sales process so that there would be no mistakes or ambiguity on the documentation for the itemized contract.

Now, it turned out that this builder who called me from Sydney was very systemized and organized too. And he'd already built a couple of apps for builders that were being sold on the Apple platform. So, he told me to check out a new online project management software. I googled the company and saw that there was going to be a webinar in three days' time. So, I registered for the webinar, which was at 3:30 a.m. for me.

On the day of the presentation, I crept down the stairs in the pitch black to power up my PC and watch a live presentation of CoConstruct hosted by the founder, Donny Wyatt. And as he took us through all the different features that this new project management software had for builders, I was mesmerized. This was truly exciting software and just what custom home builders needed. But I was also disappointed because this solution already did everything that I was trying to achieve, and a whole lot more. There was simply no point in continuing on the path I was on.

Straight after the presentation finished, I called Donny Wyatt in the United States because I knew I had to tell builders in Australia all about this fantastic new software. Speaking to Donny, I found out that there were only two builders currently using the platform in the whole of Australia and only one in New Zealand. Within ten days, I'd negotiated the rights to market and sell CoConstruct in Australia, New Zealand, and the United Kingdom. And over the next six years, over a thousand custom home builders signed up on CoConstruct, making it the number one online project management solution for custom home builders in Australia.

During this time, my daughter, Sky Stephens, was studying marketing at university. It wasn't long into her course that she realized how out of date the content actually was. We discussed the future of the internet, online marketing, and how fast it was all changing. Within a few weeks, Sky withdrew from university to focus on learning the new marketing strategies that were replacing the old-school methods.

To put these new skills into practice, we decided to start a marketing agency for residential home builders. We called that company ACRIS Services. Our company-built websites for builders functioned as a lead generation tool, rather than a static online company brochure. And we developed a CRM system for builders that they could use to follow up all of their inquiries that came through the website. We also managed Facebook and Google Ads campaigns for builders and ran search engine optimization (SEO) strategies. So, we looked after all things marketing for residential home builders, but *only residential home builders*. That's what we specialized in.

Things went well and the company grew. But we soon realized that no matter how many leads we generated for builders, some were successful while others still struggled. And the ones who struggled always said the same thing. "The leads are rubbish. I can't even get them on the phone. And when I do get them on the phone, they're cold. They just don't convert. There's no point in advertising. It doesn't work." Or some variation of that.

When we studied these two groups of builders, we realized that the ones who were successful had one thing the struggling builders did not have: a documented sales process. So, we knew that the missing link for custom home builders was sales training.

To fill that gap, on August 31, 2014, we launched ACRIS Sales Training. This service was dedicated to training and coaching builders to create a documented sales process. They then had a process to follow for every new inquiry, and that completely changed the way each builder we worked with operated. They no longer complained about the leads being rubbish, because they now had a repeatable sales process, and they knew what their conversion rates should be at every step of that process. As a result, they started generating more contracts than they had ever managed before.

We felt we'd solved the biggest challenge that builders were complaining about in the marketplace. We now had the solution for custom home builders who struggled to generate leads, as well as for those who were struggling to convert their leads into sales. However, although these builders were now generating more contracts than ever before, a lot of them were still struggling. They now had sales, but they still had very little time or spare cash. They were signing plenty of contracts, but they weren't signing them at the right margins.

These builders were in reactive mode and were constantly chasing their tails. They were also signing contracts in clumps, which put enormous pressure on their building company. Overall, they were doing too much work for too little net profit, and consequently, a lot of these guys ended up on a hamster wheel where they needed more and more jobs to feed the machine. And because their margins were too low, they could not afford to employ the people they needed to do the work for them, which meant they ended up doing the work themselves.

Really, they were no better off than before, when they had no leads and very few sales. These guys deserved to be earning far more than they were drawing out of their building companies, and their clients deserved a far better service than they were experiencing. A lack of systems was causing problems for both parties. So, in 2015, we launched the Association of Professional Builders (APB) with a goal to improve the industry for both builders and consumers through systemization.

And now, Sky and I have written this book, compiled from our years of experience working with custom home builders.

THE ROADMAP FOR THE BOOK

In this book, we're going to share with you the systems that successful professional builders across Australia, New Zealand, Canada, and the United States are implementing into their building companies. These builders are able to generate more leads and close more sales at higher margins, while also improving the client experience. The chapters have been divided up into three sections covering leads, sales, and margins.

PART 1: LEADS

In this first part of the book, we will give you the strategies and the systems for generating quality leads. Quality leads will come to you because your prospects see you as the only viable solution to their problem, rather than the rubbish leads who use you as a free quoting service. We will share with you the strategies not only for attracting quality leads but also for scaling up your lead generation by using paid advertising profitably. We call that *scientific advertising*.

PART 2: SALES

In part two of the book, we cover the sales systems that we've been implementing into custom home building companies since 2014. We will provide the complete sales process for a custom home building company, including the inside strategies that will enable you to take more of your opportunities all the way through to a contract.

You may not think of yourself as a "salesperson," and that's okay. There are no high-pressure, hard-sell tactics in this book. These strategies are ones that every single residential home builder can implement into their own business without being pushy or salesy.

PART 3: MARGINS

In part three, we will give you the systems for pricing your jobs and growing your margins. We will go through the entire process of how to plan for profitable growth so that you can scale your custom home building company safely and securely. We'll also show you how to increase your margins by using the law of *supply and demand* to your advantage. By engineering more demand for your services than you can hope to supply, your building company will actually become *booked out*.

WHO THIS BOOK IS FOR?

This book is for you if:

- You're the owner of a residential home building company.
- You've been told that it's not possible to add 33 percent profit to your materials and labor.
- You're simply working for wages, with very little in the way of net profit left over at the end of the year.
- You've been told, either by other builders or by consumers, that you can't charge more because you simply won't win the job.

This book will show you why the things you've likely been told are simply not true. It will also include examples of builders who have implemented these strategies and changed their building companies, as well as their lives.

If you've been in the industry for a long time and you're skeptical that anything in this book will work for you, then you're probably right. In our experience, builders over the age of fifty-five are resistant to new ways of doing things because they've been conditioned to working a certain way through over thirty years of exposure to the industry. For these strategies to work for you, you have to be willing to make some changes in your building company.

A lot of builders come to the Association of Professional Builders because they have just started a new building company. They have seen what has happened to others in the industry, and they want to avoid the pitfalls that might result in their business failing, too. They want to do things correctly right from the start. If that's you, you are exactly where you need to be right now. If you follow the strategies in this book, you will go from strength to strength at a rapid pace, without ever having to experience what most builders in the industry have had to endure over the years. You are in the best possible position.

For those of you who have been in the industry a bit longer and are finding yourself spinning your wheels and getting frustrated, this book has the answers that you've been searching for. It's not too late to turn things around and take your building company to the next level. And please know that all those years it's taken you to get to this point are not wasted. They have given you the experience and the knowledge that will provide the platform for you to take your building company to the next level simply by following the strategies in this book.

So, let's get started.

PART 1:

LEADS

CHAPTER 1:

MARKETING FUNDAMENTALS

*You have less than 15 seconds to capture
someone's attention on your website.*

— TONY HALE, *CHARTBEAT*

In 2010, when I was selling workplace health and safety documentation, I traveled out to meet Michael, a builder in Brisbane. In an attempt to make a bit of conversation and build rapport, I said to him, "So, what is it you do?"

Michael looked at me like I was completely stupid. He said, "I build. Building is building, isn't it? It's all the same." He was quite astounded by the question, which told me exactly where his business was at.

So, when I asked him, "How's business?" I already knew the answer.

Straight away Michael said, "It's crap. The margins are crap. And it's tough to get any sort of work at the moment. I've got an architect who refers me to his clients, but all the other inquiries that come through are a total waste of time. All anyone wants these days is the lowest price, and I just can't compete with some of the prices that they're quoting me." He went on, saying that it was just way too hard these days.

Now, this builder's problem was that he was trying to appeal to everyone in the marketplace. And when you try to appeal to everyone, consequently, you end up appealing to no one.

WHY YOU NEED TO ESTABLISH YOUR NICHE

It's really important to establish the niche that you're going to operate in. Especially in construction, there are generalists everywhere, and those guys are all desperately chasing any work that they can get their hands on. When builders try to appeal to absolutely everyone like this, their service becomes a commodity. This is because the only thing that separates them from another builder quoting on the same job is the price.

Now, consider how other industries work. For instance, if you needed eye surgery, would you go to a general practitioner or would you seek out a specialist in the niche? I think we all know the answer to that. With eye surgery, we clearly understand the value of someone who specializes in doing exactly what we want.

It's exactly the same for builders. The builders frantically quoting any kind of plan that gets offered to them are busy spending their evenings and weekends pricing those jobs for free. These guys are going to price anything that they get asked to price, whether it's new homes, renovations, or extensions in the hope of winning about one in five jobs.

Meanwhile, the professional builders who are focused on a particular niche are attracting the clients who want the exact service that they provide. These people are effectively the eye surgeons of the construction industry, and they are paid a premium for providing their service.

As a custom home builder, your goal is to be number one in your niche. By way of example, if I asked you who was the first person to fly across the Atlantic solo, you'd probably be able to answer that quite easily. It was Charles Lindbergh. But what if I said, "Who was the second?" That gets a bit harder because not many people have heard of Bert Hinkler. But, if I asked you who was the third person to fly solo across the Atlantic, you may not know the answer at first. But when I told you "Amelia Earhart," you'd be very familiar with the name.

And the reason we know her name is because she was the first woman to cross the Atlantic solo. What that shows us is that if you can't be number one in your niche, then you have to target a sub-niche. Contrary to popular belief, when you do this, there will *not* be less opportunity. Instead, there is actually going to be more opportunity because your sales funnel is going to convert far better when you are number one in a smaller niche than number two, three, or four in a bigger niche.

> A sales funnel is a term that describes the steps that a prospect has to take in order to become a client or a customer. Essentially, the funnel outlines each step of their journey until they sign a contract.

So, the first thing you have to do is identify the niche that you want to operate in. And to do that, you need to look at your past jobs and really analyze what you've been doing over the past few years.

- Which jobs really went smoothly?
- Which ones did you most enjoy doing?
- Which ones generated the most net profit?

As you analyze your jobs, sort them in descending order based on net profit margin. What you'll probably find is that 20 percent of your jobs generate 80 percent of your net profit. When you look closer at the 20 percent, which jobs did you enjoy doing the most? That is where you want to niche. This is the type of job that you want to be focusing all your efforts on attracting more of.

It's likely that if you have been doing a range of jobs, then you've probably been doing new homes of different levels. You might have been doing high-end custom homes, as well as more standard custom homes around about the $600,000 range. Maybe you also had a couple of small renovations mixed in as well.

What surprises builders when they analyze their past jobs is that even though they might enjoy doing the high-end custom homes, the net profit can come out quite low. Those jobs go on for longer, they're more complex, and they can have more cost overruns. However, the $600,000 custom homes are a lot simpler. Builders can generally increase their margins on those jobs' progress from cost underruns and by finishing them earlier than planned in the schedule.

Renovations are also extraordinarily time consuming compared to new homes. Builders can easily find themselves losing money on these jobs if they're working on the same margins as a new home. So, when you look at it, you think, *Renovations, yeah, we're plugging a gap in our workflow and picking up turnover.* But, in a lot of cases, you're not actually making any net profit from them. The high-end custom homes are great for marketing, and for image, but they're not very profitable when you are a generalist. Instead, if you homed in on those $600,000 custom homes, you could do a lot more of those and make a lot more money at the same time.

EXAMPLES OF HOW TO NICHE

Again, get really clear on your niche before you move on to anything else. One example of a broad niche is *custom home builder in [location]*. If you can own that niche in your local market, then obviously that's a great brand. And just as obviously that's going to be quite competitive, so you might have to sub-niche.

Custom homes vary from around $500,000 to over $20 million, so your niche could be a certain level of custom home. You could niche into architecturally designed custom homes and target the higher end of the market. Or you could go the other way and target the affordable custom home sector.

You could also come at your niche from an angle of the timeline. Custom homes completed within x months. Again, you'll target a particular price range of homes so it's less complex.

Another example could be something highly specific like sloping blocks, especially because a lot of building companies don't want to touch those. If you become the specialist in sloping blocks, then if a consumer has one, they're going to be drawn to you as the expert in that niche.

Once you're clear on your niche, you then need to determine the type of person you want to attract. This is something we call the *ideal avatar*.

WHY YOU NEED TO CREATE YOUR AVATAR

If you try to appeal to everyone in the marketplace, you're going to appeal to no one. Your niche is going to get the attention of the entire marketplace looking for that particular service. But when you market to your ideal client, otherwise known as your avatar, that will attract more of the people that you want to build for while also repelling the people you'd rather avoid! So, who is your ideal client for your particular niche service?

In this exercise, you need to look at your previous clients. Again, look at your jobs over the last few years and think about the types of clients that you enjoyed working with.

What were their demographics? Age? Married or single? Kids?

Consider location. It's not just a case of where you're prepared to build. Where are your clients located right now? They might be moving from out of state or even from another country, so take that into account as well.

Look at their occupation. What do they do for a living? What industry are they in? At what management level? What's their income level? If you're building high-end custom homes, then you're probably going to be dealing with the top 1 percent. If so, you need to add that income level to your targeting.

Take into account their building experience. Are you targeting first home buyers, or people building their third or fourth home?

What are their desires? Why are they choosing to build? What's the common thread in what consumers are looking for?

What are their fears about construction? If they've not built before, what are they concerned about? What is it they don't know about building? If they have built before, is there an experience that they're concerned about repeating? Get really clear on what their pain points are.

What are their interests and hobbies? Where do they like to go on holiday? What motivates them outside of business?

Look at the marketing channels that are bringing these specific people in rather than just your overall leads. You're looking at where your best clients come from. That's even more important than seeing the source of the majority of your leads.

Once you've completed that exercise, you then want to look at your problem clients. This is probably a much easier exercise because when you look at the problem clients with the benefit of hindsight, you can normally see the red flags that were there all the time. Maybe you ended up taking on the job because you needed the cash flow, but there are always clues. Make sure that you identify the traits of the problem clients. You can then use them as disqualifiers in your qualifying process.

So, once you've gone through that first exercise, make a list of all the attributes of your ideal client. Create an avatar and then give them a name. Typically, in this industry we think of the primary person as a couple. And since it's usually the wife initiating the inquiry, that's who we really want to appeal to. But we're also speaking to the spouse as well. They're both going to be decision-makers, so we want to make sure we're talking to both of them.

Your avatar could be Business Owner Bob, for instance, married to CEO Cindy. Whatever the traits are, give your avatar a name that resonates with the typical ideal client. If you end up with more than one avatar, that's fine. But for now, just focus on creating your first one. Get really clear on their attributes, give the couple names, and write a few paragraphs about them. And whenever you do anything in marketing, make sure you have your avatar in mind.

In the future, whenever you write your sales copy, you're not going to be writing generally or talking about the features of your building company and what you've done, and so on. You're going to write directly to this avatar couple. And when you shoot a video, visualize speaking to them.

WHY YOU NEED TO ESTABLISH YOUR BRAND

The third thing you need to be doing in marketing is establishing your brand. Branding is believed to have been started by the ancient Egyptians back in 2700 B.C. when they branded their livestock. They did this in order to differentiate their cattle from other farmers', which meant stolen cattle could be easily identified.

These days, despite branding being an *intangible asset,* as we call it, brands are now worth millions of dollars. But good branding is about more than just your logo. Your brand is a representation of what your company stands for and believes in. It's the voice that your company speaks with and the tone that it uses.

Your branding *is* your marketing because it represents everything about your company, such as who you're targeting and the service and benefits that you provide. It also reveals your positioning in the marketplace. For example, high-end or low-end. It becomes your style, and even your audience. Making a brand synonymous with an audience is something that Apple did really well in the early eighties when they wanted to attract more of the same people.

Ultimately, the value of a brand is determined by how it's perceived in the marketplace. We can measure our clients' perception of our brand by implementing the Net Promoter Score survey and by looking at online reviews. The higher the ratings, the more a brand's value increases. Typically, when we value companies, we look at the net profit and then apply a multiple to give that company a value. The brand value is then added on top of that initial valuation. It's an intangible asset, but it is very important.

This applies to every single business because your brand is what differentiates your building company from every other builder. And without it, you're just like Michael, that builder in Brisbane, who was trying to appeal to everyone in the hope of getting as many jobs as possible. He didn't have a brand, and without one, you are simply a commodity—which is why he didn't have any net profit either!

To build a brand, you need to deliver a consistent experience for every single person who comes in contact with your company. To do that, it's very important that you do three things.

- Establish your marketing messages. These messages include your unique selling proposition, your niche statement, and the benefits of the service you provide. Your marketing messages are a direct representation of your brand and will deliver a consistent experience across your marketing.

- Establish brand guidelines. Create a style guide so that when anyone does any marketing or design work for your building company, your brand will stay consistent. In order to establish value, you must have consistency.

- Establish your company culture. To do this, you need core values that you truly believe in and live by every day. This will keep your company culture consistent, which will keep your brand experience consistent as well.

FEAR OF MISSING OUT

So, by now you might be wondering what became of Michael, the builder in Brisbane without a niche. After we spoke, did he follow my advice and turn his company into a very profitable residential construction company?

Well, I could tell from speaking to this guy that he wasn't going to change his mind. The United States Coast Guard has a great saying: "We can only help the ones who swim towards us." And at the Association of Professional Builders, we have a similar saying. So, I set him up with the workplace health and safety documentation that he wanted and wished him all the best for the future.

Sadly, after I'd left, this builder continued doing the same thing as he'd always done, all the while expecting a different outcome. That's the very definition of insanity, according to Albert Einstein. But five years later, in 2015, just after the Association of Professional Builders had launched, he did reach out to us for help. And during the discovery call, the APB Executive Coach quickly identified Michael's biggest problem: he told him that he didn't have a niche.

The coach spoke with him about this in depth, about how in trying to appeal to everyone, he was appealing to no one. And Michael said, "Yep, I get it. But, if I limit myself to just one niche, then I'm going to lose out on all the other potential work." The way he saw it, things were getting tighter and tighter every year, and he couldn't afford to miss out on anything. So, he declined to take our advice and carried on doing what he was doing, while expecting a different result.

If you're ready to do something different to get better results, first take some time to determine your niche, and then your avatar. You can also go to the resource section of our website, www.apbbuilders.com/pbsbook, to download a worksheet for marketing your building company. And once you're clear on these marketing fundamentals, you'll be set to tackle content marketing in the next chapter.

CHAPTER 2:

CONTENT MARKETING STRATEGY

Content is King.

— BILL GATES

Recently, we've been watching a Spanish television series called *Money Heist* on Netflix. In it, a team of thieves takes over the Spanish Reserve Bank with the plan to steal the gold that is stored in a secure vault under the building. (Spoiler alert, if you haven't yet seen the series.)

As part of the security measures, as soon as anyone attempts to break into the vault, the chamber will fill up with water. Therefore, these thieves have to concoct a plan that enables them to extract the gold from a flooded vault. But it's not just the gold that they're interested in. On the far side of the vault, behind a plain wall, lies a second vault. So, the question is, what on Earth could be more valuable than a nation's entire gold reserves? The answer is: its secrets.

Marketers have been claiming for a long time now that information is more valuable than gold. Just ask Cambridge Analytica, the company behind the Facebook privacy scandal in 2018. They've been using information to decide elections all over the world for years.

This is why the real intangible value lies in a building company's secrets. Not the dirty little secrets it is trying to conceal from the taxman, but its industry knowledge. The knowledge that builders freely give away in the form of advice to prospective clients during their one-on-one chats can be exchanged for the number one thing every business needs to survive: attention. By sharing your knowledge, your experience, and your advice, you will get the attention of your target market. Attention leads to interest, and interest generates new leads for your building company.

Take a moment now to think about what your marketplace needs to know. What are the most frequently asked questions that you or your team are being asked? When you answer those questions and make the information available to your ideal client in the form of content, it will be worth its weight in gold. It will transform your building company from being a commodity to becoming a professional service. And that's the secret of how you avoid competing on price.

CONTENT MARKETING TO THE RESCUE

A content strategy is all about using information to get leads. By attracting the attention of your ideal client, you can convert them from a reader or viewer into a lead. An example that really shows the power of this strategy is APB member Ryan Stannard from Stannard Family Homes. Towards the end of 2019, we organized a content strategy for him, which was going to really propel his building company to the next level.

We all like to think of growth as a straight line, where sales and profitability go up. But business just doesn't work like that. Business grows with a series of S-curves. This is a sequence of S's stacked on top of one another. What it shows is that in order to grow to the next level, your profitability will initially drop back before recovering and growing. Ryan was already a real action-taker. He was always moving forward, and not at all afraid of the S-curve (see *Figure 2.1*).

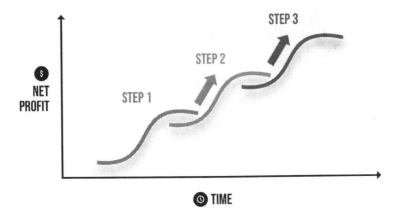

Figure 2.1: The S-Curve

Ryan knew that each time his current structure hit a ceiling, he would have to go backwards in terms of profitability to break through it and power forward. In early 2019, he had completely committed to advertising, and had started to see good results. But Ryan was champing at the bit. He was eager to scale up even faster, so he engaged us to develop a content marketing strategy for his building company.

By February of 2020, Ryan's content strategy was ready to launch—just as COVID-19 was about to hit. So, Ryan had invested all this money into a strategy just as one of the biggest black swans to hit our industry in the past seventy years was about to descend upon us. Would Ryan's investment be a total waste, or would content marketing get him through this?

THE IMPORTANCE OF A CONTENT STRATEGY

Implementing a content strategy is probably one of the most powerful things you can do for the long-term health of your building company because it creates awareness, generates quality leads, and builds trust. It also helps to convert more of your opportunities into high-margin contracts, which also increases net margins.

Now, when you look into producing all of that content and embarking on a full content marketing strategy for your building company, it can appear daunting. But if you leverage the content that you create correctly, you can really amplify your efforts. The thing to remember in business is that small hinges swing big doors.

By that I mean that one single piece of content that might take you twenty minutes to outline can be used to produce a blog article for your website, a content video for YouTube and Facebook, an email campaign containing three emails, and fifteen unique social media posts for Facebook, Instagram, and LinkedIn.

We do this all the time for a small number of select builders that we work with. When we go through the process of content creation, it takes no more than a couple of hours of the builders' time to discuss their ideas—then we go away and do all the work in the background. All they have to do is approve the finished content, and, of course, turn up to the film studio for a couple hours of filming to produce the videos.

At the end of this process, the builder has twelve months of high-quality content for less than a few hours of work. This process is highly leveraged, and it protects the builder's time. The next section will detail the process we use and that you need to follow to get the maximum value out of the content you create.

A NOTE ON COPYWRITING

When you embark on a content strategy, don't scrimp on copywriting. This point is extremely important because words convert website visitors into new inquiries far better than images. So, you may need to bring in a contractor who specializes in copywriting and understands our industry.

If you've got a marketer to run your team, they're probably not going to be the best person to write the content. The marketer will be great for overseeing the project, but copywriting is a different skill. It's like comparing the work of a skilled carpenter to the work of an unskilled laborer who has an interest in woodworking. If you go with the unskilled laborer, you're likely going to end up with a poor end result that will hurt your building company's reputation. You've got to invest in a skilled copywriter to create the content based on your brief.

HOW TO STRATEGIZE CONTENT

In the process that we've developed at APB, we start with a brainstorming session to identify topics to write about. This is the most important part of the process, so think of it like when you start a build and how critical the slab pour is to your future success. You spend so much time and energy making sure everything is just right because you know that if you get it wrong, you're going to be constantly making adjustments to compensate for that flawed slab.

Put the same amount of effort into the brainstorming session so that you don't have to keep making corrections to the content as it is being created. The best way to do this is to get a blank piece of paper and divide it into four quarters by drawing one line vertically down the middle and another horizontally across the center.

STEP 1: BRAINSTORMING

Write a heading at the top of each quarter, as follows: FAQs, Features, Pain Points, Process. These are topics that you will need to brainstorm with your team. Don't dig deep into each one at this stage. Just get them down on paper.

FAQs (or Frequently Asked Questions)

It's really important to bring your team in on this one particularly. The sales-people will have a great idea of the questions they get asked most frequently by prospects, as well as the questions that come up later in the process. Get all of them down.

Features

What are the big features of your particular service? What's unique about your building company? These are great topics to write about as well.

Pain Points

Think about your ideal client and the avatar that we spoke about in the previous chapter. What are their pain points? Get those down on paper.

Process

Finally, what's your building process? It is extremely useful to outline the process your company goes through to design and build a custom home, both for people who haven't built before and for those who've had a bad experience in the past.

Once you get all these topics down on paper, you'll then refine them. From your refined list, choose the twelve best topics. What are the most important things that you need to be talking about? You can cross out the ones that are further down the list or keep them as topics to use when you repeat this process in a year's time.

STEP 2: PAIN POINT SOLUTION

The next step is to dive into each topic in a bit more detail. You will need a separate piece of paper for this.

For each topic, write down a very broad description or an overview of the pain point from the customer's perspective. And then write your new idea for solving this particular challenge for the consumer.

Give your solution a unique name to ensure you really own it. Then, go on to describe the solution. Limit yourself to three tips or steps as this works the best in our experience.

For example, a question that gets asked a lot is: "How long will it take?" Consumers get really concerned about this because the longer the build process, the more their holding costs rack up. They want to know that their home will be built within the timeframe that the builder claims. The best way to address this concern is by including a guaranteed completion date in the building contract. So that could be the solution's unique name, *Guaranteed Completion Date*. And we would start referring to that as a professional term. We would then come up with three tips, as follows.

Tip #1:

It's the construction start date that matters. Your completion date has nothing to do with when you sign the contract. So, you can be under contract, and what you'll find in the fine print is that the contract won't activate until work starts onsite. When building companies are busy, they'll often sign contracts without committing to a start date, and as a result they sit on contracts for six months or more. So, make sure you have a guaranteed start date included in your contract before signing it.

Tip #2:

Make sure you have a real point of contact. An office administration person is a buffer who can't make decisions without speaking to the supervisor. If you want to avoid delays and get answers quickly, make sure you've got a dedicated point of contact who is regularly onsite and can make decisions.

Tip #3:

Use a builder with an online client portal. An online portal allows you to track the progress of your build 24/7, rather than going to the site in person and trying to figure out if it's progressing or not. With an online system, you can easily make sure that progress is on track.

Obviously, you'd put a bit more meat on the bones for each of these tips, but that gives you an example of what's included.

STEP 3: THE COPYWRITER CREATES A SCRIPT

It's important to have the copywriter involved in this entire process because they need to have an in-depth understanding of the topic that they're writing about. They'll be able to ask questions all through the process to really understand your perspective and make sure that they can deliver a top-quality article for you.

It will probably take about ten to twenty minutes to create the copywriting brief for each topic. When you finish, the copywriter will then be able to go away and put together a high-quality script for you. The more preparation you put into steps one and two, the more likely the writer will be able to absolutely nail the script the first time.

Once the script is complete, all you need to do is approve it. And when you've got all the scripts written, you can then go into a studio and record them all in one go. Or, if you prefer, you can just record them on your phone. But the thing to remember here is that sound is critically important. It's more important than the actual video itself because sound is what will lose people when you're amplifying your content to a wider audience. This is why we highly recommend using a studio for recording your videos.

You now have twelve content videos that you can use as part of your content marketing strategy, and this is where it gets exciting. Because, with minimal effort, you can really amplify your content strategy by getting your copywriter to adapt the script into a blog article for your website.

STEP 4: COPYWRITER ADAPTS SCRIPT INTO BLOG

It won't require any major changes to turn the script into a blog post. Subtle changes to wording will be required because instead of speaking to a camera the text is being read in the form of an article. But one of the most important things the copywriter will be doing here is inserting subheadings.

Blog subheadings cater to the skim readers, or the people who glance through quickly to get an idea of what an article is about. In a lot of cases, they'll then go back and read it in full if it seems worth their time.

The copywriter will break the article up into subheadings, and they'll also insert some images to break up the article. That way, when it appears on your website, it doesn't look too overwhelming and text-heavy. By inserting a few images, maybe three or four, the article will become more visually appealing and easy to read. So, in addition to the twelve videos that you can use on YouTube and Facebook, you now have twelve articles for your website.

The next thing you can do to really maximize this opportunity is to break each of those articles into three sections. You can then use each one of those sections to create an email campaign.

STEP 5: BREAK BLOGS INTO EMAILS

The three sections from the blog will all be part of one email campaign that is broken up into three different emails. We will string them together using what we call open loops. That's where the story breaks off partway through to leave people on a bit of a cliff-hanger. That way, they're eagerly awaiting your next email in the sequence.

This is something that has been used on television for decades now, and it's how all of those mini-series operate. They leave you in suspense so that you're excited for the next episode. An email can work exactly the same way. So, we open up a loop, leave them on a bit of a cliff-hanger, and then close the loop on the next email.

Now, in addition to your twelve videos and twelve blog articles, you have twelve email campaigns each containing three emails, or a total of thirty-six emails, added to your digital assets. And to take this a step further, using this content that's already been created, your copywriter can then go ahead and produce at least fifteen social media posts from each article, just by repurposing short extracts.

STEP 6: CREATE SOCIAL MEDIA POSTS

The beauty of repurposing everything like this is that you don't need to keep approving each social media post because you've already approved all of this copy or text. The writer is simply reusing information by breaking it up into fifteen social media posts.

One post could be a quote that you used as part of the article, another could outline a pain point and a short video clip could outline one of the tips. This would give you a nice combination of images and video in your feed. Even the images selected for your blog article can be used as part of this strategy. Now, you have 180 social media posts in addition to those thirty-six emails, twelve blog articles, and twelve full-length content videos, which means you've created your assets.

The next step is to schedule everything. You can't just push it all out into the marketplace and think, *Job done. Thank God that's over.* It's very important that you get the launch right and that you space out the release of your assets into the marketplace in order to generate maximum impact from them.

STEP 7: SCHEDULE EVERYTHING

We recommend releasing a new topic each month, and also tying your topics to the seasons, if that makes sense. So, in month one, you'll be releasing an article on your blog and publishing the videos that relate to that article on Facebook and YouTube. And when you do this, make sure you add closed captions to your videos since a lot of people will watch your videos with the sound off.

Luckily, adding closed captions is very easy to do. Plenty of third-party services online will do them for you very cheaply. You just provide them with the video, and they'll create the captions in a compatible format to accompany your video posts.

Your email campaigns will be scheduled in your CRM, and you can plan on releasing a new campaign every month. You might decide to release an email every day or every couple of days. You might prefer to do it every week, but that's probably a little bit long for this style of email with the open loops. Ultimately, the choice is up to you, but we recommend releasing another email two to three days after the previous one.

Next, schedule out all your social posts. And with the 180 social posts that you've produced from this strategy, you can schedule a new social media post every two days for the next year. Then you're done. It really is as easy as that.

CALLS-TO-ACTION (CTAS) AND LEAD MAGNETS

Once you've got all this great content out into the marketplace, it isn't going to generate leads for you on its own. You still need two vital components, and they are CTAs and lead magnets. We use a CTA at the end of an article, which will then take the reader to our lead magnet.

A lead magnet is something of value that you give away in exchange for an email address. What you're really after here are opt-ins. For example, someone will see your post on social media. From there, they'll be taken to an article on your website. When they get to the end of the article, they'll see the CTA, and they will opt in to your CRM system by providing their name and email address to receive the lead magnet that the CTA offered. Now, you have a lead on your database.

At least, this is how it works in theory. It's not always that simple. These three steps don't always happen at once, so getting someone to opt in can take a bit of retargeting. Your social media posts might get people to read your articles, but they won't necessarily opt in the first time.

When we use the strategy of retargeting, we retarget those people who read the article or clicked through to view the article on our website but didn't opt in. That's how we maximize the opportunity. It doesn't always happen in one bite, or even two, but that is the general principle.

It's very easy to create your own lead magnet because it's going to be on a topic that resonates with your particular audience. So, if you're a design and build company, you might be giving them design tips as a lead magnet. Again, we recommend using a copywriter to produce this once you've got the ideas laid out.

And then, you just need to produce your landing page, thank you page, delivery email template and an ascension email campaign. You can deliver it all through your automated marketing funnel.

Your landing page will get people to opt in for your lead magnet, and the thank you page is what they see once they've opted in. The thank you page confirms that you've received the person's details, and that the lead magnet will be sent to them in the next few minutes. Typically, this is where you make your next offer in order to progress your prospect to the next stage in your sales process.

Your delivery email will typically send the lead magnet straight to the email address they provided when they opted in, and then ideally, your ascension email campaign will begin. This is a campaign consisting of three emails, with the same goal as your thank you page, to progress the prospect to the next step in your sales process. Typically, the next step in the sales process for a residential home builder is to book an initial consultation over the phone.

THE TRUE VALUE OF CONTENT MARKETING

Now, to get back to Ryan Stannard, who back in February 2020 invested a great deal of time, money, and energy into producing content assets just as the industry was facing its biggest challenge since the outbreak of World War II. It wasn't looking good for Ryan in the beginning. There was a lot of uncertainty facing the industry. He even wondered if all that cash he had just invested in content creation might have been better off being held in reserve.

However, what happened next was the exact opposite of what anyone expected. His inquiries went through the roof because of his new content. The reason for this was simple. As households went into lockdown, they had more time to go online and do research. And what were they searching for? Information! And Ryan was the builder providing it.

So, consumers consumed his information. Then they opted in to his database. And while every other builder watched their existing sales pipelines disintegrate, Ryan was having some great sales conversations with new prospects just entering the marketplace.

Unlike other builders who would eventually have to rely on government stimulus packages to prop up their sales funnels, Ryan's sales started to grow from day one. In the middle of a global pandemic, he signed more contracts in quarter two of 2020 than he had ever signed before. As a consequence, he ended up having to take on more staff in quarter three to cope with the extra work.

In short, Ryan's business took off in a time when almost everyone else in the industry was struggling—all because of his content marketing strategy.

Now that you see how incredibly valuable content marketing can be, in the next chapter we'll go into the benefits of paid advertising and how to use it most effectively. But before you turn the page, we'd suggest going to www.apbbuilders. com/pbsbook to download our Content Ideas Swipe File, a handy guide for thinking more about your own content ideas.

CHAPTER 3:

USING PAID ADVERTISING TO SCALE UP

Stopping advertising to save money is like stopping your watch to save time.

— HENRY FORD

You cannot scale a business purely based on referrals or on content marketing alone. To get real growth, you must use paid advertising so you can create more awareness of your building company in the marketplace. This will bring more people into your space who will potentially turn into paying clients.

Advertising has changed quite considerably, especially over the last ten years—with the internet changing the whole buying process. In all industries, the traditional method of just putting up an advert with a phone number to call no longer works. We need to be a lot smarter these days, which means we need to use good quality information in order to educate the market.

Now, the good thing is that it's never been cheaper or easier to promote a building company. But it does require a good content strategy with good quality information, like we outlined in the previous chapter. Then, you can use paid advertising to promote that content. If you don't pay to promote, which we call *amplifying*, then very few people are going to see it—especially on social media where organic reach has dwindled over the years to minuscule levels. If you want people to see all the great content that you're putting together, paid advertising is your only option.

However, be aware that paid advertising generates cold leads. Builders often make the mistake of assuming the next step in the sales process is just like dealing with a referral, which is what we call a warm lead. Leads from paid advertising do not convert as well as warm leads because these people know nothing about you; they didn't shortcut the research process by getting the recommendation from a friend or family. Cold leads are much more skeptical, and they need to be warmed up through education.

That said, just because the ratio of cold leads that converts into clients is a much smaller percentage than warm leads, this doesn't mean that advertising doesn't work. It also doesn't mean that you should only focus on warm leads. In truth, these cold leads convert profitably when you follow the right strategy, as the following story shows.

LOST IN TASMANIA

Matt Smith ran Rainbow Building Solutions in Tasmania, which is a little island off the south coast of Australia. He came to us because he was struggling to generate leads. He was spending over $30,000 a month in radio advertising to promote his new home building company but without any proper strategy. Following previous "just get your name out there" advice, he was using the traditional advertising methods like, "Give Rainbow Building Solutions a call at xxx-xxx-xxxx." He spent $30,000 a month on this type of advertising, and it was bringing in very little in the way of new leads. In fact, one campaign that Matt ran cost over $10,000 and failed to produce a single lead—not one!

Matt knew he couldn't just rely on referrals. He knew he needed to advertise to grow his business, but he didn't know how to do it successfully. The more he spent, the more frustrated and desperate he got. He knew advertising had to work—otherwise, why would every successful building company advertise? But he just couldn't seem to figure out what to do or how to find anyone to help him, until he found APB.

ADVERTISING METRICS

Online marketing is the most cost-effective way to increase awareness of a building company. Television, radio, and print advertising used to be the only options available, and they were expensive, which is why so few building companies actually used them. But online advertising is affordable for every single business, whether they're national, international, or even local. And it's incredibly cost effective to get an online advert in front of not just an audience but your ideal client. That last part is really important.

So, online advertising gives you the opportunity to target very specific people. You're not wasting your money like you would be on television, radio, and in print by advertising your services to people who have no interest. However, when you use online marketing to promote your building company, you must analyze your numbers. You really need to understand where the money is being spent, what it's being spent on, and the return on investment (ROI) that you're getting.

If you use an advertising agency, in all likelihood, they will focus less on the metrics beneficial to you and more on metrics beneficial to presenting a case that they're doing a very good job. In truth, they're probably building up awareness from people who are never going to build, ever.

So, there are two main metrics that require your focus when acquiring a new lead:

- Cost to acquire a lead.
- Cost to acquire a sales qualified lead (SQL).

Now, most advertising agencies will focus on the cost per click, and that is a meaningless metric for a multitude of reasons. First of all, Facebook did an in-depth study on this and they've proved there is no correlation between people who click and people who buy. What they actually use is another metric called landing page views, which is slightly different to clicks. Regardless, those mean nothing to the business owner when it comes to lead generation. They're metrics useful only for measuring an awareness campaign or for an agency to present to you because, when you see high volume, it looks like they're doing a great job for you.

The number one metric a business owner needs to analyze is the cost to acquire a lead. Usually this is calculated per channel or even per campaign. To do that, you simply look at how much you've spent and then you divide that amount by the number of leads you generated through that campaign. An important note, however, is that in order to do that, you need to have your tracking set up so you know where your leads are coming from (ad tracking is a small piece of code that can be installed on your website or landing pages such as a Facebook Pixel or Google Conversion Tracking so that when a user clicks on your ad the data can be collected in your ad campaign).

The second metric is often overlooked, and a little bit further down the funnel: the cost to acquire an SQL. Similar to getting clicks and landing page views, leads can be a little misleading. Calculating the cost of a lead is the best metric to focus on in the very beginning, but as you start generating more volume, you'll want to go further down the funnel and start looking at the quality of those leads. The way we do that is by studying how much it costs to acquire an SQL.

SQLs are potential clients who match your qualifying criteria necessary to progress to a contract. That transition will be typically done by your sales team and it requires a phone conversation. We'll get into all that in the next chapter. Right now, we're just looking at the basics like: are they actually looking to build? This is an important question because you will get people opting into your funnel who are not prospects and are only looking to get a foot in the door in an attempt to sell you *their* services. Or they might be other builders trying to see what you're doing from a marketing perspective.

Another basic question is: where are they looking to build? If someone isn't looking to build in your footprint, then you won't be able to service that lead. It's automatically disqualified.

Purely looking at the first metric (cost per lead) can be very misleading. When you get to speak to these leads and qualify them, you'll then look at how much you've spent divided by the number of SQLs and that will give you the cost to acquire one SQL. That's a very important number to know, because the conversion rates for SQLs to contract compared to leads to contract are a lot more stable across multiple channels.

As an industry benchmark, you can make the assumption that one in ten SQLs will progress to a contract. If it takes more SQLs to sign a contract, then there's something wrong with your sales process or with your qualifying process. If you convert more than one in ten of your SQLs into contracts, then you probably have a very strong presence/reputation in the marketplace. There are many other factors that will contribute to your conversion rate going up. But if you're not converting at least 10 percent of SQLs, it points to problems in your sales funnel.

COSTS WILL VARY

Now, there are a few anomalies you need to be aware of here. First of all, the cost per lead will vary by channel. But the cost per SQL will be pretty even across all the channels. Facebook advertising for instance is interruption marketing (which we'll explain shortly). You're interrupting people who might be in the early stages of considering whether to design and build a new home while they're doing other things, like looking at friends' profiles. Whereas another channel, like Google Ads or even SEO, delivers more committed leads because they've come from a related search for a builder. For the purpose of this example, when we say Google Ads, we are referring to paid search rather than Display or Video Ads.

How Google Explains Paid Search:

"When you type something into Google, you are presented with a list of results; or SERP (the search engine results page) which shows organic results and paid results.

Paid search results have a little green box with the word 'ad' before the listing; this is where a company, like yours, has paid to have their page show up at the top of the list. This can be done through Google Ads search campaign, which charges you when someone clicks on that link. Paid search works to drive traffic to your website through relevant ads." (Source: Google Ads)

You'll typically pay more for a lead that comes in through a Google Ads search, compared to a lead that can be generated by Facebook. However, when you qualify your leads properly, you'll discover that regardless of how they come into your funnel—SQLs are SQLs, and they pretty much all convert at the same rate from that point on.

In terms of what you should be spending to advertise your building company to promote it, there are a variety of theories. Most of the numbers you hear being thrown around are general and apply to many different industries. The construction industry, however, is unique; it has very high turnover and low net margin, and you need to be aware of that. As a good guide, keep in mind 1 to 3 percent of your *target* revenue. This isn't the revenue that you did in the last twelve months; it's the amount of revenue that you're planning on doing in the next twelve months.

This is because you're generating future sales. If you focus on investing the amount of advertising it will take to generate the leads to produce the contracts that you did last year, that's exactly what you'll get. But if you're looking to grow, for example, to increase the business by 50 percent, naturally you'll need to ramp up your advertising spend to achieve that.

Look at your budget for the next twelve months. You'll need to budget between 1 to 3 percent of that revenue just on advertising. That doesn't include any of the services to manage Facebook, Google, or YouTube advertising—just the ad spend itself. And it doesn't include other general marketing costs either, like your website or blog articles and landing pages. How much you invest will really depend on how aggressive you're getting in the marketplace.

If the average contract that you're signing is $500,000, then you can probably expect to pay between $500–$1,500 per SQL. Bear in mind, this is returning to the idea of ten SQLs being necessary to produce one contract. Now, if it takes ten leads to produce one SQL, then that means you can expect to pay between $50–$150 per lead generated. That's where you want to be in order to make these numbers work. That's what you need to be looking at in terms of your cost per lead and your cost per SQL.

But again, be very aware that some channels are considerably cheaper than others when generating leads. And of course, the lead quality will also vary. It might take a lot more Facebook leads to generate one SQL. And in a channel like SEO where they're searching for you or your services, they will be a lot more qualified—so it'll take a lot fewer leads coming through that channel to produce one SQL.

For instance, you could be paying $25 per lead on Facebook, but only one in twenty of those leads are SQLs. And from your SEO strategy, each lead could be costing you $100; however, one in five of those leads are SQLs. The end result is that the SQLs are costing you $500 each regardless of the channel. And that's the reason why it's so important to keep an eye on both of those metrics.

CLASSIFIED VERSUS INTERRUPTION ADVERTISING

There are two types of advertising. There's what we call classified advertising and then there's interruption advertising. Imagine flipping through a magazine. The classifieds involve many sections with a structure that allows people to find exactly what they're looking for, such as a plumber, electrician, or a builder. Interruption marketing is mixed throughout the content of the magazine, so it can grab people's attention a lot earlier in the buying journey. They're not actively searching for a particular product/service/professional in the classifieds at this moment in time, but subconsciously they are open to the idea of building a new home or starting a large renovation project.

Interruption marketing gets you two results. First of all, as mentioned, you'll reach prospects a lot earlier in their journey and get to speak to them long before any other builders. Secondly, the leads you generate through interruption marketing are typically a lot cheaper. Conversely, those leads are less likely to convert. It's another reason why we look at the cost per lead and then the cost per SQL, because that's the point at which it becomes a level playing field.

How does online advertising apply to classified and interruption marketing? Google Ads is the modern version of the classified ads in the back of the magazine, whereas Facebook and Instagram are the equivalent of interruption marketing within the pages of that magazine. Regardless of the strategy, you need to have both good content and lead magnets, like we covered in the previous chapter.

As established, on Facebook and Instagram, people are probably not ready to start looking at a company's brochure, or even design ranges, at this stage. But you might attract them with a free guide or a checklist. Their subconscious might be exploring reasons for them not to build, because for instance, friends of theirs recently built a home and it was a horror show. The goal is to tap into that mental conversation at a very high level, very early in the buyer's journey (five things you need to avoid if you're building a new home, seven things you need to know before designing a new home, etc.).

Google Ads, however, works differently because the lead is already looking for a builder because they have a problem they're trying to solve—they want to build a new house. They want to speak to a builder to solve their problem, so they're solution aware. In terms of a lead magnet, the strategy we would use is to get them to opt in for a company brochure, design range access, or even a price list. These work really well on Google Ads because the lead is a little bit further down the funnel than those that are being targeted on Facebook and Instagram.

To say it another way, when the leads are further down the funnel or further along in their buyer's journey, Google Ads is definitely a good place to start advertising.

Once you get your ad campaigns working and you have what we call *proof of concept*, then you have proved that your sales process is good enough to convert cold traffic into paying clients. It's one thing to have a sales process that can get people that have been referred to you over the line—it's quite another to be able to do that with people who know nothing about your building company. This is where a documented sales process comes into play.

If you don't already have a documented sales process, you can download the Sales Blueprint for Builders at www.apbbuilders.com/pbsbook, where the entire process is outlined out for you.

A successful sales process is very easy to accomplish when you follow something that's already working for other builders. Once you have that in place, then you can convert paid leads into contracts. From there, you can progress into SEO.

An effective SEO strategy requires you to optimize your targeting of keywords around the words that have already been proven to work in a paid search. Keywords are nominated words or phrases that best describe your organization, products, or services. In other words, a word or phrase that a user types into a search engine when they're looking to find your business but may not necessarily know your business name. And typically for an effective SEO strategy, there are several words or phrases that are possibly similar in nature but use different combinations to ensure your business will appear in the results, whatever the user is searching for. For example, someone might type in *New homes San Diego* or *Builders San Diego*.

When you spend money on a Google Ads paid search, the aim is to rank at the top of the search results. That way it is more likely that people will start opting in to receive your lead magnet offer and eventually convert into clients. So, when that happens, you know you have keywords that convert well.

The next step is to start ranking organically in Google, Bing, and the other search engines for those keywords. Ranking organically means that when people type in a search term, not only does your company appear as an ad at the top of the search results, it also appears near the top under the paid ad results that appear. And those who click on the organic listing are the best leads you can possibly get (a) because they're free, and (b) because they are more likely to convert into clients compared to the leads generated from paid advertising. So, once you have your paid search strategy working in Google Ads, then you'll want to consider investing some money in SEO to rank organically for the keywords that convert. If you do it the other way around, you'll waste a whole lot of time and a lot of money. On that, don't waste your time doing SEO yourself! Pay a professional to do it for you—but proceed with caution. We'll come back around to this at the end of the chapter.

GETTING STARTED

Start with one channel and get that working. If you try to do too many things at once, you just end up spinning your wheels creating chaos and confusion along the way. So, get that one channel working before progressing onto the next.

We recommend starting with Google Ads because they are hot leads and it's relatively easy to get prospective clients into your funnel because they're already searching for a builder. Now, that isn't always ideal because it can also mean they already have their designs finished and are just looking for more quotes from other builders. But, if you're set up to provide a design and construct service, then you can target people searching for designs, which would mean getting them earlier in the buyer's journey. Which is why we suggest that Google Ads is a good place to start in terms of paid advertising because you can test out your sales process quicker.

Then we recommend moving on to Facebook and Instagram, and finally SEO. Overall, SEO takes the longest to really get working. To invest in SEO, you don't want to waste your time hiring cheap companies overseas offering their SEO services for a few hundred dollars a month. They'll probably cause more harm to your online presence than good. You need to invest in an SEO professional to get productive long-term results that compound over time. That's not cheap in the early months. Which means you'll get a much faster return on your advertising dollars by investing in Google Ads, then Facebook and Instagram, before trying to get SEO working as a strategy.

For each of these channels, don't spend your own time and energy doing it yourself. There's a lot to learn and the tactics are always evolving and changing, so it's not very easy to keep up with the latest information on what's working now. It's best to use a professional to provide this service so you can focus your time on doing the things that will propel your company forward.

Purely in terms of the hourly rate involved—it's not worth your time, so outsource. Once you're working with a professional, you need to be very clear about your expectations. You're not looking for clicks but for actual leads. That's how you'll measure and define success. Make sure you're working with people who understand this and will deliver reports on what they've been doing in line with what you need to know and what you expect from them.

The bottom line is that outsourcing is just like having employees. They might be contractors, but if you think, *They're the experts, I'm going to leave it to them*, you'll burn a lot of money over time. What gets inspected gets respected. You need to be watching everything that they're doing and reporting on it. And no, not just looking at their reports, you need to be reporting independently as well. At APB, we have a saying: *We trust, but verify*. We would never accept a report from a contractor without verifying the numbers through our own reporting to confirm that those numbers are real. This is mainly because people make mistakes.

LESS IS MORE

Back to Tasmania! Once Matt discovered the APB and started working with us, we showed him the process for using paid advertising, just like we've outlined for you here. It was all about using content marketing at the very top of the process, so he could then attract the right people—high-quality leads.

When Matt followed our strategies and implemented this process into his own building company, he spent money promoting useful information rather than simply promoting his name and phone number. Then he started advertising a downloadable item that offered value to his prospects. In some channels, that was a free guide on designing a new home. In others, leads were able to download a plan range and a company brochure. Once he started doing that, his leads increased very, very quickly.

It was only a matter of months before Matt's lead generation went up to over two hundred leads per month. While accomplishing those numbers, his advertising spends actually decreased from $30,000 to $21,000. So, he spent less money advertising his building company, but his lead generation absolutely exploded.

However, the thing that really moved the needle for Matt came after the leads were generated. There was a bit of qualifying, and a bit of discovery. And we'll cover that in detail in Chapter 4. In the meantime, go to www.apbbuilders.com/pbsbook to download the Facebook Pixel and Events Placement Checklist.

PART 2:

SALES

QUALIFYING LEADS

*The price of success must be paid in full,
in advance.*

— BRIAN TRACY

Now that you're starting to generate more and more leads, the next most important part in the process is qualifying those leads. We'd like to frame your thinking around this process with a story that originally comes from Perry Marshall, the well-known business strategist.

In this story, a young gambler is taken under the wing of an older, more experienced gambler in Las Vegas. As part of the training, the experienced gambler takes the kid to a real seedy joint downtown. The experienced gambler nods towards the poker table, where eight people are seated, examining their cards. Without saying a word, he pulls out a sawed-off shotgun from under his coat and he racks it beneath the table. It makes that loud ratcheting sound that only someone familiar with shotguns is likely to recognize.

Three of the eight people at the gambling table look around, then look back down at their cards. The older gambler turns to the kid and says, "Those are the three who you do not want to gamble with. Your marks are the other five." And that's what Perry Marshall calls *racking the shotgun*. It's a way of qualifying or disqualifying a segment of people in order to identify the best possible prospects.

In terms of overall qualifying, there are three different levels that a builder needs to implement. There's the initial qualifying stage, then the discovery stage, and then the targeted prospecting stage. The last one is all about timing, because people's circumstances change. In the next section we'll explain how to go through the process of the initial qualifying so that you don't waste your time on the wrong people. This ensures that you're progressing only the right people through to a discovery call and following up with only your ideal clients.

QUALIFYING

As a kid, you may have had one of those puzzles with different shapes cut out. The goal was to teach you to put the round peg in the round hole and so on. Because if you tried to put the round peg into a square hole, for example, it simply didn't work. No matter how hard you tried, you could not force it into the hole.

It's exactly the same with qualifying your prospects. If you get the wrong type of prospect, it doesn't matter how hard you try and how good your offer is, you're never going to get that prospect to sign a contract with you. You will end up wasting a hell of a lot of time on the wrong type of people, which is why it's so important to qualify your prospects quickly. Once you know that you've got a round peg, you know that it has the potential to go through the round hole and on to discovery. But when someone isn't a good match, and won't pass through your filter, you need to disqualify them and let them go.

A lot of builders think that they can't afford to say no to potential clients. They need every potential contract they can get, no matter what type of project it is, and no matter who the client is. They believe they have to try to close every single opportunity. But the truth is that 80 percent of your problems will come from 20 percent of your clients. And when you ask the right questions, you can identify these problem clients. Then, you can disqualify them, and they will become someone else's problem.

The initial qualifying stage involves closed questions, and because of that it is a lot quicker and shorter than the discovery stage. You just need to determine if these people are going to be a good fit for your building company or not, and that you are going to be a good fit for them. In other words, that you are not trying to put a round peg into a square hole again.

You can figure all of this out rather quickly by asking four to seven non-negotiable questions. That means that if you get a particular answer, that client has to be disqualified without emotion, no matter how badly you need the job. Asking the following questions can uncover your non-negotiables:

SEVEN QUESTIONS THAT BRING UP NON-NEGOTIABLES

Question 1: What prompted you to reach out?

The best question to start off with, to warm the conversation up and to get a real feel for their background, is to simply ask, "So tell me, John, what prompted you to reach out to us today?" What you're trying to do here is to very quickly establish a link between your marketing and this inquiry. But this question will also alert you to reasons they may not be a good fit.

Prospects who inquire without knowing anything about your building company have a lower probability of progressing to a contract. So, what you're really looking to discover is how warm they are. How much do they know about your company? They might say, "I've been following you on Facebook for six months." That's a great thing to uncover!

What you don't want to hear is, "I've got plans drawn up, so I did a search on Google, and your name came up." (Along with ten others!) That's a disqualifier. Don't waste time with someone who comes to you on that basis. To them, you're just a builder who's going to quote their plans, which means they're going to make a decision based on price. You want people who make decisions based on value.

Question 2: Where are you looking to build?

Like we mentioned in Chapter 3, don't spend too much time qualifying people who aren't building within your footprint. If their land is too far away, or you simply don't have the infrastructure in place to service that build, you can cut the conversation short very quickly.

Question 3: Have you settled on your land?

If they are looking to build, they need land, so ask about that very early on. It's going to be a presumptive question. You're assuming that they've got land lined up. But if they're just looking for land at this stage, then they are a good prospect for your database only. We'll come back to how to make sure these prospects do not fall through the cracks later. But right now, until they've got land, they can't even begin to think about a design.

Question 4: What type of home are you looking to build?

Does what they want fit with what you offer? It's very important that the people who come to you are looking to build the type of project that you specialize in building. That's how you offer value. It's what separates you from the rest of the market and helps you win jobs and increase your margins. If you build homes in the $1 million plus range, you are not going to take on an investor looking to build a box for under $200,000. Apart from anything else, you're not going to be able to compete on price with the volume guys who are geared up for this type of work.

Question 5: Do you have designs drawn up?

What you're looking to do here is establish how far along the buyer's journey these people are. And if you're a design and construct company, you shouldn't be wasting your time quoting plans that are being shopped around to six other builders.

However, there may still be opportunities for a redesign in the future because most likely, the design they have was either drawn up from an architect or a building designer, and therefore most likely doesn't have the input of a builder and is going to be over their budget. So, it could be a potential lead for the future. However, right now they don't realize the pain they are about to experience trying to get the budget to meet their design. So, it's not a good immediate-term prospect for a design and build operation, which is a business model that every residential home builder should be considering moving into.

Question 6: Who will be involved in the design process?

Who's going to be involved? You need to know who the decision-makers are. For a design and construct company, you'll want to establish the names of the stakeholders and involve all of them in the design process. That will enable you to avoid being blindsided later in the design phase when someone else suddenly enters the decision-making process.

Question 7: When are you looking to move in?

Most consumers have very little idea of how long the whole process of design and construction is, so they often delay getting started on the design process thinking they have more time than they do. Just knowing the target move-in date for them enables you to work backwards and use urgency in your follow-ups. "If you want to move in by _____, we need to get started on _____!" Just beware that if the prospect has no deadline or urgency, you could be doing a lot of work for someone who lacks the motivation to progress their project or to see it through to the end.

So that's our initial qualifying process. These questions should help you identify who's a good fit for your building company, and who's a bad fit. And if you find yourself in a situation where you can't let go of the bad fits because you don't have enough good fits, the problem lies elsewhere, most likely with marketing and advertising. The problem is not with the questions you are asking.

Coming up next is the discovery part of the process, where you'll go a lot deeper with your questions. This is where you will really start to build rapport and trust, and demonstrate authority.

THE VALUE IN DISCOVERY

Sam Bernardo was a custom home builder in Victoria, Australia, who really had the discovery process nailed. A great example of this is a story from back in 2019, when he found himself dealing with an exceptionally cautious couple. The budget for their new home was over $950,000, and this was going to be the first home that they'd ever built. So, they were inexperienced in the whole building process and were particularly nervous about what they didn't know that they didn't know.

They'd heard all the horror stories out there about what could go wrong, so the thought of giving a builder the best part of a million dollars was causing them to procrastinate. When we're not sure if we're doing the right thing, our instincts are to do nothing. And that's what was happening with these clients.

In addition, as a lot of people do, these clients were speaking to two other builders about their project. However, Sam had an edge over the other two builders competing for the work; because he had invested time in the discovery process, he knew exactly why the couple was procrastinating. And because he understood their concerns, he also had a system to address them. We'll come back to his system at the end of the chapter, once you're more familiar with how the discovery part of the process works.

THE DISCOVERY STAGE

An important thing to remember throughout the discovery stage is that we're transitioning from closed questions into open questions. This is not an insurance form or a tick and flick. We don't want it to come across that we're just going through a series of questions.

Because you've already done the initial qualification, you know that the prospect is a potentially good fit for your building company. It's now very important to invest some quality time with them and really go deep on every single question. The most important aspect is to really listen to their answers. You've got two ears and one mouth, so use them in proportion. You should be talking less than 33 percent of the time.

An interesting added benefit is that the less you speak, the more interesting the prospect will find you. Generally, the more people speak about themselves, the more interesting they find the person listening to them. It's counterintuitive, but it really does work. For some people, listening isn't an easy skill to master. So, a good tip for this, while you're still practicing, is to hit the mute button on your phone. This will help you to avoid the number one mistake builders make: talking too much.

Remember that the discovery phase is all about the prospect. If you've done your marketing correctly, they already know all about your services, features, and benefits. This is 100 percent about getting to know and understand them.

Instead of jumping in or thinking ahead to what you're going to say next, take the time to listen and think about what they're telling you. Then go deeper by following up on their answer. Don't move on to the next question until you've thoroughly exhausted the current one. If you go deeper, you can get them to reveal what they need from you so that they feel more comfortable with the process. The goal is to find out what motivates the prospect because that will be the difference between them choosing you over someone else.

The following question is often a good one to start your conversation. It focuses on getting to know as much about the prospect as you can. Then, you can move on to the other questions.

DISCOVERY QUESTIONS

Have you built before?

If the answer is yes, then there's a high chance this person is going to be realistic about their budget. But you still need to go deeper by asking what they liked about building their previous homes. And when they answer, it's just as important that they reveal exactly what they didn't like.

It's also helpful to know which consumers have never built before because there's a good chance they have some unrealistic expectations regarding budgets. This lets you know to put a lot more focus and education on the budget part of the process.

Why do you want to build a new home, rather than move into an existing one?

Ask the question and then pause. Let them answer. What you're trying to do here is uncover the emotional drivers behind this decision because the emotional drivers are what will help you to win this job. If you can uncover the real motivation behind them wanting to build their own home, that will be a key piece of information in the months to come when you are progressing the opportunity into a building contract.

Is there anything that concerns you about the building process?

You've got to understand what keeps the prospect up at night worrying when it comes to building a new home. And when you understand their pain, you can make sure to overcome that objection in any future dialogue. Every time you talk to them, you want to move their project forward, and for them to want to move ahead to the next stage, they need to feel completely comfortable and confident with you and your process.

What's the most important thing to you about the build process?

People build for different reasons. Some are all about the quality. Others just want to move in before Christmas. And some might be on a tight budget. But generally, it will be one of those three things: quality, speed, or budget. And you need to understand which one it is while still keeping the question open. If they respond with something like, "Getting what we want," then dig deeper. You can say, "Tell me more about that." Keep going until you find the real driver.

This question will really determine the direction you take with the advancement of the sale. If someone is building their third and final home, they may want it to be just perfect. So budget is less of an issue. But for someone on a tight budget, you'll want to give them options to bring down the price. And of course, if they have friends or relatives coming from overseas for Christmas, then the timeline is a non-negotiable. So, you need to make sure they see you as the only builder who can guarantee they will be in their new home before Christmas.

Who else have you approached regarding this project?

It's important to know who you're competing against. If the prospect has built before, are they talking to their previous builder? If they had a good experience previously, then you're probably being used as a price-check. It doesn't mean you are going to give up on the prospect since they're qualified and overall a good fit. But you can make sure to match the other builder's weaknesses against your strengths and emphasize your strengths in order to highlight their weaknesses. Make sure you do your research here to avoid spending months working on a project that you never had a chance of winning.

What are you looking for in a builder?

With this question, you can find out what's important for them in a building company. Their answer will also tell you how they would like you to sell to them. So, whatever they tell you they're looking for, make sure to highlight those details as your strengths in your proposal document. And make sure that you can deliver on what they need.

Keep in mind that you should be at least forty-five minutes into the conversation at this point. Only then do you move on to the budget question.

How much are you looking to invest in this project?

A lot of builders will ask about budget as an initial qualifying question. "What's your budget?" The problem with asking that question so early on is that you have no rapport at that stage. So, if they do give you a number, it's unlikely to be the truth. And in a lot of cases, they know what they want, but they don't know how much it's going to cost them. A volume builder might have told them, it's $x amount per square foot. And based on that, they're going to tell you a ridiculous number.

If you disqualify people because they've given you a low budget, or they don't know their budget at all, you are missing out on a lot of opportunity. So, we recommend only discussing the budget once you have built rapport and know they are a good fit for your building company. Be careful not to put them on the spot because if they really don't know, they may just throw out a number and the conversation could go south. For this reason, go ahead and present some price ranges based on what they have already told you about the project.

Are they looking to invest over $1 million, $600,000 to $800,000, or less than $500,000? See how they self-select. Because despite all the listening you've now done, you still may have misread the situation. You may be thinking, *It's going to be a $650,000 build,* but instead they could say, "We're looking to invest over $1 million."

When you throw out price ranges, it also allows those on a tighter budget to state their limit very clearly. "No, we cannot go over $452,000." But what if, based on everything else you've learned in the discovery process, you know that their budget needs to be in the $600,000 to $800,000 range? If you know that $452,000 is unrealistic, you can have that conversation with them right then.

"From what you've told me, it's simply not going to be possible to build the type of home you want on that budget. People will tell you that they can design that for you on that budget. But you're not going to find a builder who will sign a fixed price contract without any allowances at that price. Which means you'll end up going back to the drawing board to make the design fit the budget, which means you'll end up wasting a lot of money on design fees."

Dig deeper to see if that really is the absolute maximum they can go up to. If so, what are they prepared to compromise on? Let them make that decision. Regardless of what they decide right now, you're building more and more trust because you're having that conversation with them.

If you've reached this point in the discussion and you're only twenty-five or thirty minutes in, you've simply not gone deep enough. You haven't found out enough about them. It's easy to say, "Well, I can't spend an hour with every person who makes an inquiry!" But the reason we do the qualifying questions first is to make sure that we've got a round peg going into a round hole. We're investing an hour of our time only with people who are qualified. So, this is time well spent. If your competition is only spending ten or fifteen minutes with these people, who do you think is in the pole position to earn their trust? It's going to be you.

It's also important to follow up with the people who were disqualified during the initial qualifying call based only on timing issues. Maybe they didn't have their land yet, or their timeline was just too far into the future. You want to make sure that those people stay in your CRM system and you follow them up. However, marketing alone won't always draw these people to you at exactly the right time for them. And that is why we recommend using a strategy called *targeted prospecting* as part of a follow-up process. We'll talk more about this in the next section.

FOLLOW UP WITH TARGETED PROSPECTING

If you are not following up with prospects in your database every ninety days, you are leaving money on the table. You have invested a lot of time, money, and effort in acquiring these leads just to let them slip through your fingers. These are the people you are not actively talking to because their timeline did not fit your criteria. However, people's circumstances change.

It's all about timing. And in most cases, the couple who didn't have land six months ago won't be reaching out to you once they've found it. But they will respond to whomever contacts them next, whether that's you or your competition.

Targeted prospecting is simply retargeting your database by phone, SMS, and email. It's just like retargeting people who have visited your website but didn't opt into your database. You retarget those people to get them to advance to the next step.

If you do your marketing right, you will also attract people who are not quite ready to talk to you at the very early stages. And that's fine. Those prospects will enter your database, and you can educate them through your content so that when they are ready to have a conversation, they are far more familiar with your brand, your story, and your processes.

Getting people into your database before they're ready to commit means you are investing in the future of your business. But you do need a bulletproof process for following them up. That includes email marketing, but it also involves retargeting them by phone and SMS.

However, you don't want to clutter up your CRM system with opportunities that are not advancing. So, when a prospect appears on your radar as an opportunity, but after contacting them you discover that the timing isn't right—there can be a reluctance to mark those deals as *closed lost*. You might think, *Oh, but they will have land in six months. I'm just going to flag them and follow up then.* However, this seriously distorts your sales pipeline and leads you into a false sense of security. At some point you end up kidding yourself into thinking you have thirty great opportunities, and if you convert just 20 percent of them, you'll have six contracts.

Do not delude yourself about these prospects. Those opportunities are dead at this moment in time, and you must reflect that in your CRM system so that you are not wasting too much time on them. A way to do this, without losing the opportunity for good, is to use the targeted prospecting strategy. A targeted prospecting strategy involves making an outbound call to every lead on your database that you have a phone number for, who has not been disqualified and who is not currently flagged as an opportunity, every ninety days.

Which means, every ninety days a prospect will get a phone call asking them a very simple question based on the information that has already been gathered. "Hey, John, are you still looking to build a new home in Toronto?" Or "Are you still looking to build that investment property in Brisbane?" Phrase this question according to your niche and the service you provide.

You probably won't get through to 70 percent of people. In those cases, you'll have to leave a message, and that's fine. It's another touch point, which we'll talk more about in the next chapter. But 30 percent of people will answer. And for every twenty calls that you make, one person is going to say to you, "Wow, that's great timing. I'm ready to talk right now." Perhaps they settled on their land and were talking just last night about contacting a building designer. It will leave them thinking, *It must be fate!*

When your database is qualified, you'll get this response from about 5 percent of the people you speak to. And this will generate opportunities that have a 10 percent chance of progressing into building contracts. So, as you can see, this strategy generates a lot of business for members of the Association of Professional Builders. For every two hundred leads with a phone number on your database, you're going to generate a building contract that would otherwise have been lost to your competition.

The trick is that you must use this process in conjunction with the content marketing strategy that we outlined in Chapter 2. This is because you have to keep your database warm for this to actually work. Otherwise, you are cold calling rather than contacting targeted prospects, which results in far fewer quality conversations.

SAM BERNARDO'S SYSTEM

Getting back to Sam Bernardo's story, he had a system that he'd been using for quite a few years. He had a library of email templates covering every aspect of the design and build process, and he'd been systematically sharing this information with every prospect who joined his database, every week. So, while his competitors were ignoring the needs of potentially high-value clients who were feeling completely overwhelmed by the prospect of building a new home from scratch, Sam educated them about the process, every step of the way.

Sam understood that the clients were nervous and he knew the reasons why because he'd listened to them during the discovery process. And he didn't assume that they were going with another builder, or that they had gone cold on him. He knew the reasons behind their procrastination. And that's why he kept reaching out to them and keeping the opportunity warm.

Clients were absolutely amazed that Sam took the time to not only educate them and alleviate their fears but also to reach out by phone periodically to see if they were ready to move forward. That made them feel wanted because he was the only builder who did this. And they really appreciated the fact that Sam kept sending what they called *some great advice*.

Of course, the system Sam used was completely automated. But this didn't matter to the client. Their perception was that Sam was providing a personal service and delivering good information that they needed to overcome their anxiety so they could get started on building their dream home. And the end result was a very welcome $950,000 contract, as well as a client who now viewed Sam as the industry expert. This was about to make the whole process go even more smoothly because both the builder and the client were on the same page.

In the next chapter, we will present some strategies for following up in the sales process and advancing the sale, including ways to overcome common objections. In the meantime, go to www.apbbuilders.com/pbsbook to download the Builders Qualifying Checklist so that you're all set to start the process for properly qualifying your leads.

CHAPTER 5:

FOLLOWING UP IN THE SALES PROCESS

*If you don't have a sales process ...
you'll become part of your prospect's
buying process.*

— JEB BLOUNT

We need to start off with a word of caution here. It's important to think of the services that you provide as being the foundations of your building company. The delivery of those services is what everything else is based upon. So, as you ramp up your sales, you need to make sure that you have a systemized building company that delivers a great service. Because if the foundations are not strong enough to support growth, increasing your sales is going to put too much pressure on your building company, and it's going to give way under the strain. The company will eventually fall over.

What you are discovering in this book is powerful stuff. And if you don't deliver a great service, then you'll be the one who suffers along with your clients. There are no shortcuts in business and no easy fix button. Scaling up a building company takes a lot of commitment and hard work.

If you know that you need to implement more systems to streamline the delivery of your services, then you should focus on that before you start investing energy into ramping up your sales and marketing activities. In the next section, we'll show you why following up your prospects is so important.

THE PRICE OF NOT FOLLOWING UP

Robert's story is an example of why following up is so important. Robert is a custom home builder who has been operating for over twenty years now. We'll explain at the end of the chapter how he made it through this patch, but it was a rough one. This was back in 2009, when things started to go downhill in the residential construction industry. Robert was still generating a lot of leads, but not converting them. And things just got tougher from there.

At his company's peak, Robert had a sales manager and three other salespeople working for him. But one by one, he had to let the salespeople go. Finally, he just had the sales manager, Jane. And ultimately, when things didn't improve, he had to finally let go of Jane and take over all the sales himself. This meant that Robert was now responsible for calling all the leads.

So, one Saturday morning, Robert sat down with his spreadsheet listing all the leads' contact information because he didn't have a proper CRM system. He pulled out his phone and started working down the list. As he did, he was astonished at the number of clients he spoke to who said, "Oh, I've already signed a contract. I didn't hear from Jane, so I went with another builder." And he had a massive realization that his company had been slowly dying over the last twelve to eighteen months simply because the salespeople hadn't been doing their jobs.

They'd contributed to the demise of his company by ignoring one of the most fundamental principles in sales: you must follow up. Because if you're not following up, then you can't influence the outcome and maximize the opportunities that you're spending thousands of dollars generating through your marketing efforts.

COMMON PROBLEMS WITH FOLLOWING UP

There are a few core principles that you must follow in business and in your sales process when you're following up. One of the main problems we see with builders when they follow up is that the prospects are very difficult to contact.

When you call them, you end up getting their voicemail, because fewer and fewer people answer their phone now if they're not familiar with the number calling them. Getting emails into people's inboxes can also be very difficult. It's easy for your email to go unseen by the recipient.

And the worst thing that can then happen is that builders tell themselves people aren't responding because they are not interested. Maybe they've decided not to build, or they've decided to go with another builder. Or maybe the prospect just didn't like them, or they were using them as a price-check.

We tell ourselves these lies because we're trying to avoid rejection. This is why a lot of the time we simply avoid following up with people. We don't want them to reject us, so we let them slip through our fingers. And there's a big harmful myth out there that says, *the leads that don't chase you are rubbish.* That is simply not true. You must avoid telling yourself those stories, because when you do, you lose out to your competition.

THE 3X3 STRATEGY

The best way to avoid missing out on these great opportunities that you're generating is by following what we call the *3X3 strategy.* Follow this process for every new lead that hits your database with a phone number. The 3X3 strategy is all about making three attempts to contact a prospect using three different channels. In total, that equals nine attempts to contact a person through phone, email, and SMS.

When you use the 3X3 strategy, speed is absolutely critical because success in sales is literally measured in seconds, not minutes. And definitely not hours or days. So, the moment you get an inquiry with a phone number, you've got to make that outbound call instantly.

A lot of builders will tell themselves that they don't want to appear desperate, and they'll leave an inquiry there for a day or so. But all that does is demonstrate to the prospect that the builders don't care about them. And meanwhile, the competition has jumped straight on the phone and is now speaking to the prospect and has started building rapport.

This is how a lot of the myths about poor quality leads come about. Because by the time these builders do reach out, the lead is already talking to another builder who has demonstrated more professionalism and care in their service. At this point the lead might say, "Oh, I'm not interested at the moment. Maybe in a couple of months," or "I'm just looking." If you hear this, then most likely they are brushing you off because they've already built rapport with the professional builder who called them back instantly.

This is something that applies to every business, even ours. As an example, we have a great member, Tye Alroe, who still remembers how he followed us for over a year on Facebook before he was confident enough to reach out. But when he finally did reach out, the thing that still sticks in his mind all these years later is that we contacted him within seconds. So not only were we successful in reaching Tye because we contacted him straight away, particularly when the subject was so fresh in his mind, but we also managed to leave him with a lasting impression.

The 3X3 strategy does require that you have an email address and a phone number for your contacts. So do keep in mind that it is most suitable for the leads with both methods of contact. The first thing you do when someone submits their phone number is give them a call. Even if they've already gone ahead and booked in for a consultation, or a meeting with you in a few days' or a week's time—it doesn't matter. You still want to make that call instantly, to confirm their booking. This is really important. And if you call and you get their voicemail, don't worry about that. It happens all the time. But what you don't do is leave a message. You should hang up, and then instantly call back again.

Now, when you do this, you will significantly increase the number of conversations that you have with people. It has become a default process for all of us with mobile phones that when we get an incoming call, and we don't recognize the number, we just let it go to voicemail. But bang, when that number calls back, you find yourself thinking, *Oh, this is important.* And in a lot of cases, the call will get answered.

This is a strategy that we use ourselves at the Association of Professional Builders. As an amusing sidebar, one of our salespeople got caught out using it. He phoned, and on the second call, the builder answered and said, "What?" Our team member replied with, "Oh, hi. It's Dave from APB." And the builder said, "Did you just call me?" And Dave said, "Yes, we practice what we preach! This is what we do." Then the builder said, "And that's what annoys me about you, Dave!"

It's usually best that you never admit to a prospect what you're up to. You are better to just say, "Yeah, I don't know what happened there, it just cut out.

Anyway…" and you move on to take control of the conversation. Now, a lot of builders who we speak to don't want to do this, and that's fine, because it makes it easier for the others to succeed. So that's the first tip that we'll give you.

When you call back the second time and there's still no answer, then that's when you should leave a message. And it's very important that your message is concise and to the point. We'd recommend following a script like this:

> *Hey (prospect's name), it's (your name) from (your building company). I'm calling you today in regard to (reference their last action). No need to give me a call back as I'll be heading into client meetings for the rest of the morning/afternoon. What I will do for you though, is send over a quick text message/email containing a link to my personal calendar so you can book a time that's convenient for you and I will call you back then.*
>
> *Talk soon.*

Once you've left the message, instantly send an SMS stating that you've just tried to call them and have left a voicemail. This is because some people might only play their messages at the end of the day. SMS has enormous cut-through, which is why it is your second channel. After you send the SMS, also send an email. So now, you've hit them with three different channels instantly. That is going to really get the attention of someone who is serious about designing a new home.

Now, the next day, you repeat the entire process. You don't wait a week before you contact them again. If you do wait an entire week, by then they'll have forgotten who you are. They'll probably also have developed a relationship with the professional builder who did manage to connect with them, and then they'll tell you that they're not quite ready, or they were just looking. And you'll start believing the lead is poor quality. It's not. Someone else is eating your lunch.

So, you've got to repeat the process the very next day, but at a different time. If you called them in the morning, then maybe you will try in the afternoon or early evening the following day. But you're going to try the exact same process all over again.

You're going to call, and if you get voicemail, you're going to hang up and instantly call back. If you still get voicemail, you'll leave a concise message and then send them an SMS instantly. Finally, you'll send them an email as well. And that is strike two.

You've now made six outreaches to this person. If they're seriously looking for a builder, and they have the concern that most consumers have about communication, they're going to be quite intrigued at the level of communication you're demonstrating.

Now, if this still doesn't get a response from your prospect, then on day three, you're going to repeat the process again. You're not going to put it off for another week because you feel awkward or pushy. You're a professional, they have reached out to you, and now you are investing your precious time attempting to help them. If anything, they should feel awkward for ignoring you, not the other way around! So, you're going to go all in day three; however, you're going to use a very different tactic this time.

On day three, you're going to use what we call the *goodbye message*, which is the takeaway. And not only that, if you don't get a response, you're going to mark this opportunity as lost. You're going to move on. Because you're going to be safe in the knowledge that this opportunity will get picked up in a few months by your targeted prospecting strategy that we spoke about in the previous chapter.

On day three, you're going to make that phone call again. If you get voicemail, you're going to hang up and then instantly redial. And if you still get voicemail, the message you're going to leave is the breakup message, the takeaway. It's very important on strike three, that you make it very, very clear to this prospect that you will not be calling anymore. You're going to do it professionally and politely, and with the assumption that they've changed their mind and decided not to proceed. You're sorry to hear that, but you're not going to waste any more of their time, and you really do wish them all the best. For example, you could say:

> Hey (prospect's name), it's (your name) from (your company). I've tried getting in touch with you a few times now via phone, email, and SMS to learn a little more about your new project. You're obviously busy and I don't want to pester you any more than I already have, so I'll mark your inquiry as closed on our end. Take care (prospect's name), and I wish you the best of luck with your project.

What this does is create a sense of FOMO, or fear of missing out, in this prospect. And you will find that 20 percent of people will now reach out to you. They'll either call you back or reply to the SMS, or they'll reply to the email that you sent on strike three. Because all these messages will make it very clear that this is the last time you will be reaching out to them. They came to you and asked for help, and you've been professional and responded. But after nine attempts, they still haven't responded to you. Now it's time to move on and focus on someone who does want your help. This is the most powerful message you can leave.

When people don't respond to you in strikes one and two, don't get disheartened. Instead, look at it like you are simply paving the way for strike three, which has the highest chance of a response from that prospect. Really, this is another example of racking the shotgun, which we spoke about in the previous chapter. This third attempt allows you to identify the 20 percent who are serious about moving forward. If 100 percent responded, you'd be inundated with phone calls, and speaking to a lot of the wrong people. This is another great qualifying process that really helps you identify the best people.

FURTHER DETAILS (7-11, QUALIFY, AND CONTINUANCE)

Another part of your follow-up process is a very important strategy known as the 7-11 law in sales. In most cases, to get a person to progress to a buying decision, you need to have built up a level of trust and authority. And to do that, it typically takes seven hours of engagement and eleven touch points.

Everything you do is going to be a touch point. So, all those phone calls and voicemails that you left, the SMS messages and the emails that you sent using the 3X3 strategy—they're all touch points. The other part of this is the seven hours of engagement.

This doesn't mean that you have to be face-to-face with them in order to accumulate those seven hours. They could be reading your emails or information on your website, or they could be watching your videos on YouTube and Facebook. And then of course, it could include the qualifying and discovery calls they have with you, which may take about an hour. So, it's not seven hours of your time; it's seven hours of their time consuming your content. You just need to make sure that you've got the content for them to consume. In Chapter 2, we talked about a content strategy and building out the articles that prospects can consume in their own time.

When you follow the 7-11 rule, always have the mindset that prospects want to hear from you. This is because salespeople who are optimistic are 57 percent more successful than pessimists, as demonstrated by a MetLife study in the 1980s.[1] They're also tenacious. And tenacity is a key skill in a salesperson. So, if you're not tenacious or optimistic, you need to get out of sales and bring someone in who is. However, when you do bring someone in to handle your sales, make sure that you look for examples of tenacity and optimism in the interview, as they are crucial qualities to uncover.

When you do manage to speak to someone during the follow-up process, don't get tongue-tied. Instead, default straight back to your qualifying process in Chapter 4. Whether it's live chatting on your website, replying to an email, responding to an SMS message, or answering a phone call—the questions that you ask are your qualifying questions. And once you go through those, you can then transition into your discovery questions, which begin on page 43.

You always want to be advancing the sale. So, to make sure that you are doing this, whenever you're making outbound calls, always start with a pre-call checklist. The pre-call checklist should have three questions on it.

1. Why am I calling this person?

2. What do I want them to do?

3. How can I deliver exceptional value on this call?

These are the three questions that you need to ask yourself before you make any type of call, whether it's to a new prospect, a prospect that's quite warm, or to an opportunity that you are progressing towards a design agreement or even into a preliminary building agreement (PBA). It really doesn't matter where they are in the sales process. Before you make that call, you must ask yourself these three questions.

When you're making a follow-up call, you never want to say to a prospect, "I'm just checking in." Instead, you want to make it clear why you're calling them. "The last time we spoke, Joe, you said that you wanted to speak to Mary about coming into our offices this week to get started on the design process. Have you

---

1. https://www.forbes.com/sites/jimkeenan/2015/12/05/the-proven-predictor-of-sales-success-few-are-using/?sh=4d18e0b04ede

spoken to Mary?" It should be very direct. Get really clear in your mind about the outcome you want to achieve, because you're going to ask for it on that call.

And then make sure you are delivering exceptional value. "Joe, after we spoke last week, I came across an article about the benefits of double-glazing. I'll email it to you if it's of interest." Always be the person delivering exceptional value.

The thing you must avoid is something we call continuance. In sales, there are only two paths to follow: You're either advancing the sale or you're stuck in continuance. And continuance is simply just continuing the conversation. You say things like, "Just checking in," or "Just wanted to see what you thought," and the like. You've always got to have a very clear agenda to be able to advance the sale on every touch point. Many builders simply continue the conversation, while professional builders are always advancing the sale—and that's why they're in high demand.

THE 7-11 RULE COMES THROUGH

The 7-11 rule can help to remind you that you're making progress even when it feels like you're not. We've worked with builders who throw their hands up in a tantrum. "That's an hour of my life I've just wasted on that person and they didn't progress!" But no, the hour isn't wasted. They're just not ready. It's timing. When they progress in three months' time, that hour that you've spent contributed to their decision to choose your building company.

Keep in mind that a lot of those outreach hours can come from automation. A consumer can go to a website and easily spend forty to fifty minutes reading blog articles. If you have videos on Facebook, they might watch four or five of those in one go. And if you consider that each email might take two or three minutes to read, and you're sending out two or three a week—that builds their hours up over time. They're the activities that get the contact to reach seven hours of consumption, not just one-on-one time.

Now, to get back to Robert, the builder whose business was failing because his salespeople were not doing their job. Once he got over the initial shock of what had been happening, he decided to rebuild his sales process from top to bottom. And twelve months later, he received an email from a prospect who had been on his database for over eighteen months. The email read in part, "We've been getting your emails for about eighteen months now, Robert. And we're finally ready to push the button."

Their circumstances had changed, like a lot of people's, when the downturn hit in 2009–2010. But they remained on the database, and they still got the information from Robert as he continued to not only follow up by email, but as he also continued to make outbound calls every ninety days and leave messages. Which is why their message also read, "You're the only builder that we want to deal with. What's the next step?" That was pure justification for everything Robert had been doing as part of his follow-up process.

By this point, you should have a sense of how the 3X3 strategy can help convert leads, the wisdom behind the 7-11 rule, and why the content that we talked about creating in Chapter 2 is so valuable. Now that you know the kind of time and deliberation that goes into a customer's decision to buy, we'll explain how to close the sale in the next chapter. In the meantime, head over to www. apbbuilders.com/pbsbook to download the Sales Blueprint for a Building Company, which will give you a visual representation of the entire marketing and sales process.

CHAPTER 6:

CLOSING THE SALE

It's not about having the right opportunities.
It's about handling the opportunities right.

— MARK HUNTER

To maximize your opportunities and close them into contracts, it's absolutely critical that you maintain momentum all the way through the sales process. What that means is that you need to be always advancing the sale. We introduced the concept of what we call a continuation in the last chapter, which is when an opportunity is not advancing. This means the chances of them progressing ultimately into a building contract are reducing bit-by-bit every single day.

And when your prospects start going cold, their reptilian brain kicks in. The reptilian brain concept is a primal response in our brains, despite the evolution of humans over time, and it's basically our brains activating a self-preservation mode to ensure our survival. The primal instincts and behavioral patterns emerge. The reptilian brain starts telling prospects why they shouldn't progress. Circumstances can also change, and other competitors will come to their attention. Every day that passes is a danger when you're not maintaining momentum and advancing the sale. This is why it's critically important that you prepare for every sales interaction using the three questions from the pre-call checklist mentioned in the previous chapter. It doesn't matter if it's a meeting, a phone call, an email, or an SMS—always have your desired outcome in mind.

Once you've committed to always advancing the sale at each step in the sales process, the next step is learning how to close. To do so, you must be able to ask for the sale and handle objections effectively. First of all, never be afraid to ask for someone's business. It doesn't make you a pushy person. And if you can't deal with objections that your prospects raise, you're going to be left dealing with procrastinators.

PREPARING FOR CLOSING

Even when it comes to signing the actual contract, it's always a good idea to have an outcome in mind and a strategy in place, as the following story demonstrates. Now, Ryan was a very successful custom home builder and his client, Gareth, was a very successful businessman who owned a large software development company. The last few years had been good for Gareth's business, and he was now ready to embark on designing his dream home, a $3.75 million mansion set on two acres. Now, because it was such a big project, it had taken eighteen months just to get through the design process with Ryan's company. However, Ryan had been smart all the way through the process, and he'd uncovered some similarities between himself and Gareth: they had kids the same age, they were both business owners, and they both had a keen interest in fishing. So throughout those eighteen months, Ryan developed a strong rapport with Gareth by constantly tapping into these commonalities.

Ryan was an amiable, easygoing, genuine builder who could talk to anyone about anything. And he'd learned the hard way that, by keeping things light and filling the air with constant chatter, he was actually making things harder for himself. And once he realized that, he decided to make a change and so he found himself a business coach who could help him. As a result, his margins got the protection that they needed.

So, while Ryan was pretty confident that getting this particular building contract signed was just a formality, he made sure to speak with his business coach a week before the contract-signing meeting with Gareth. "There is no such thing as a done deal," his coach had told him. It didn't matter how confident he was.

Because it was such a big contract, the business coach took Ryan through potential scenarios that could come up, such as roadblocks that could delay the contract signing. They played them all out in detail. The coach had Ryan practice different strategies to deal with whatever negotiating tactics Gareth might use on the day, even though everything in the contract, down to the last detail, had already been agreed upon prior to the meeting.

All the specifications had already been documented and explained. After eighteen months of designing, quoting, making changes, and re-quoting, there were absolutely no surprises left in this contract. And since Gareth was a business professional himself, he trusted Ryan and appreciated the value and the expertise that Ryan brought to the design process as a builder. So, he had no reason to go to any other builders and ask them to put a price on the job. It really didn't seem like anything could go wrong at this point.

Gareth had requested that they meet at his office for the contract signing. Ryan arrived on time, sat down and followed the basic Business 101 process of exchanging pleasantries and building rapport before getting down to business. And when Ryan felt the time was right, he pulled out the contract. Again, he took Gareth through all the key points. He didn't take anything for granted. He went through all the inclusions and the payment schedule and then explained all the different clauses that were included as well—why they were in there and what they meant.

And then when he got to the end, Ryan said, "And if you'll just sign where I've put a tick, we can get this project started for you." And with that, Ryan placed the pen on the building contract and slid it across the desk towards Gareth. He then settled back in his chair.

But Gareth just sat there. He didn't pick up the pen or otherwise move a muscle. He just smiled back at Ryan. The silence was deafening. And the pressure on Ryan to say something, anything, just to the break the tension was intense. But he didn't buckle. He just bit his tongue and smiled back at Gareth.

Now Gareth had successfully negotiated many multi-million dollar deals in the past for his software company. This is what he did for a living. And because of the industry he was in, he'd negotiated deals with some of the toughest negotiators on the planet. For him, closing a deal with a small local custom home builder was just going to be a bit of fun. A bit like a cat playing with a mouse that had absolutely no hope of escape. So, he didn't utter a word. He just sat there staring at Ryan and smiling. And on it went.

BEING HELPFUL

Now, some builders are great at sales and others are simply terrible. And we've found that the most striking difference between successful and struggling building companies comes down to how good builders are at sales. The ones who struggle avoid responding quickly to inquiries. They avoid following up, and they avoid asking for the sale. They say things like, "Well, that's cheesy, and I don't want to do that. That's not how I want to come across to my clients. That's not how I operate, that's not me."

So, because these people would rather avoid making themselves feel uncomfortable, they will never be able to scale their building companies. Because if you can't sell, then you can't grow a business. Period. And what that means is that all you've created is a job for yourself. It's not a business that can be scaled, or even sold, in the future.

But in reality, to be good at sales, you don't need to be salesy or cheesy or even a tough negotiator. All you need to do is be helpful. This is really about adjusting your mindset.

If you adopt the mindset that you're just helping, this takes a lot of pressure off yourself. That's really the idea behind the discovery process. You can't help someone until you understand what their problem is. You talk to them, ask questions, and listen to their answers—which allows you to really understand their concerns. And then you're acting like a fiduciary, which means you have their best interests in mind rather than your own.

When you have that mindset of helping people all the way through the process, that's how you're going to be perceived by your prospect, which means you're more likely to be the builder they choose. The idea is to stop thinking about signing the contract and start thinking about how you can help this person get through the sales process and deal with challenges. If a prospect is thinking about putting a spa bath in the bathroom, being helpful could be as simple as coming across an article that reviews the best ten brands and sending it to them with a message saying, "I saw this and thought it may help you with choosing your spa bath."

Refer to the pre-call checklist on page 71. You can think of this as a variation on the question "How can I deliver exceptional value?" Instead, maybe it's "How can I help this person?" It really is the same thing.

CONSIDERATE VERSUS INDIFFERENT

The old-school methods of selling are completely dead. These days, if you don't ask for the business, your prospect will think that you don't care or that you don't want it. By trying to act like you're not desperate, you may even come across as a bit arrogant and indifferent to the other person. There's a big difference between appearing considerate and appearing indifferent, and too many builders lose out on jobs to their competitors because the other builder appeared to want the prospect's business more.

It's important to be excited about the project that you're being offered and make it clear that this is something that you would love to be involved in. And also, it's why you must always ask for the sale. Asking for the sale is not hard. There's a great book called *The Perfect Close*, written by James Muir (Herriman, 2016). In it, Muir reveals the number one thing that you need to say to close a deal, any deal. It's not salesy, and it's not cheesy. And to save you reading the whole book, we're going to share it with you here.

It's all about moving the client to the next step. When you come to the end of the meeting, and you've clearly established that they need what you're about to propose to them, and you've tackled all the potential objections that have come up because you've done a proper discovery—now the time is right for that prospect to move to the next step, and that's the only thing now for them to do.

That next step might be agreeing to come into the offices for a meeting. It could be signing up to a concept design agreement while they're in your offices. It could be progressing from concept design into a PBA, or it could be after you've completed the PBAs, moving them into a full building contract. But when you get to that point in the conversation, don't give in to discomfort or avoidance and allow the prospect to walk out of the office to go and think about it. All you need to say to get them to the next step is, "Would it make sense to_____?"

And then you just fill in the blank. "Would it make sense for you to come into our office so that I can show you through some floor plans? Then we can discuss your requirements in more detail." Or, "Now that we've got a clear understanding of what it is you're looking to build, would it make sense for us to move on to a concept design agreement so that we can get this design drawn up for you?" Or, "Now that we've got all the designs complete and we've got a good idea that we're within your budget, would it make sense for us to take the next step and sign a PBA?"

Do you see how it works? It's not salesy, and it's not cheesy. And the client can say yes or no. It's as easy as that. We've been teaching this method of selling for the past few years, and our members absolutely love it because it's something anyone can do without any advanced sales training or even the gift of the gab and also without feeling awkward.

And if you're wondering, "Well, what if they do say no? I'm stumped, what do I say next?" If they do say no, all that means is that they've got an objection. So, the next question that you would ask is, "What do you think would be a good next step?"

As an example:

> Builder: *Would it make sense for us to sign a concept design agreement so that we can get the design started for you?*
>
> Client: *I'm not sure we're ready to do that just yet.*
>
> Builder: *Okay. Well, what do you think would be a good next step?*

A lot of the time they'll probably realize that they don't have an objection at all. It was simply a knee-jerk reaction. Now, even when the consumer does have a response, you have to remember that the first thing that comes out of their mouth is generally not a true objection. It's an involuntary response to what you just said.

This is why a good rule of thumb is to actually ignore the first objection. That is, don't waste your time trying to overcome it. What you need to do is just spend some time reassuring and empathizing before you circle back and ask again, all the while expecting a positive response. Never ask for the sale with the expectation that someone's not going to move forward. You have to be in the mindset that their response will be positive. And if they don't have any real objections, that might be all that is required.

In the next section, we'll go over some of the most common objections that we see and how to overcome them.

OVERCOMING COMMON OBJECTIONS

There are at least five main objections that we hear all the time in our experience working with builders.

Objection #1: Other builders don't charge for a quote. Why should I pay you?

The first way to respond to that is to say, "Yes, that's a very good question. It's something that is very misleading in our industry, because the truth is the builders offering free quotes are really only offering free estimates."

Consumers do not understand the difference between a quote and an estimate. And to be honest, even people in our industry don't always understand the difference. You know how much work it takes to produce a detailed fixed price quote on a custom home, and you know it's not realistic to do that amount of work for free. You also know that the guys offering quotes for free aren't producing a fixed price quote like you're doing. They're delivering a one-or-two-page estimate stuffed with meaningless allowances. Of course, that's free; it has no value.

To overcome this objection, you need to empathize. Then explain the common misunderstanding and tell them that to quote a project of this size takes anywhere from forty to eighty hours of work. Then you say, "I'm sure you're already aware that no building company can do that amount of work for free and stay in business. But here's the problem with a free estimate: what do you think happens when the allowances are on the low side?" This puts the ball back in their court.

Then you say, "And that is why…" Then you outline what you provide as part of your fixed price quoting service and summarize the benefits of engaging your building company to price their project.

Most reasonable people will understand all that. They just don't know what they don't know. Of course, there will be some time wasters who are simply price checking and not interested in paying for anything, and that's fine. You don't want those people.

Objection #2: I need to think about it.

A good response is something along the lines of, "Whenever someone tells me they need to think about it, it's because the price is not quite where they want it to be. Is that part of what you need to think about?"

What you're trying to do is coax out their actual objection. "I need to think about it," basically means that you haven't addressed their concerns. You've got to drill down. If you just let people wander out and think about it, they're not going to progress unless they stumble across the answer to the objection they're holding in their mind by chance.

If you think it might be price, you could follow up with something like, "And if price wasn't an issue, is this something you'd be keen to get started on?"

What you're doing here is isolating the first objection and trying to uncover what might be the real objection underneath. And if it is price, try turning the tables on them. "Let me ask you, Gareth, how much would you like to pay?" From that, you're going to get a good understanding of the price point in their head.

Then you could say something like, "Thanks for sharing that. Let me tell you why we price the way we do and what you get for your investment."

Obviously, they're not seeing the value if they feel they need to pay less. So, break down each feature with the benefits, and then you could summarize it with something like, "You see, you get what you pay for in this industry. And I can't be more blunt than that."

If you've worked through your sales process correctly, you will never find yourself in this position because you will have managed their expectations all the way through the process. Builders most often find themselves in trouble when clients keep adding stuff and they fail to document the revised budget in writing. Then, suddenly at the end, they're $100,000–$150,000 over budget.

Objection #3: Your price is too high.

A good response to this one is, "I definitely hear what you're saying, and I'd like to work with you on this. Please help me to understand what exactly you are comparing this price to."

Now, you're going to really uncover what you're up against. Because if they can't justify why they think the price should be $200,000 less, then you know that they're not on solid ground. But you need to understand their thinking. As Stephen Covey wrote, "Seek first to understand, then to be understood."

Objection #4: I'm waiting for another quote.

Again, if you've followed the sales process correctly, you won't be quoting against other builders. But if you find yourself in a situation where you aren't the only builder quoting, then a good way to respond to that is to say, "Okay, I understand. And tell me, how will you determine which is the best quote to proceed with?"

What you're trying to understand here is how they're going to make their decision. And we know that in the vast majority of cases, consumers do not have the skillset to compare two different quotes. The only thing they'll be able to compare is the price. So, they will sheepishly admit, "Yeah, we're going to be looking at the lowest price."

And this is where you refer back to the discovery questions that we went over in Chapter 4. This is why the qualifying process is so important. If you record all the information you get from the consumer, you can use it not just for that moment in time, but all the way through the sales process. If you find yourself in this situation, reference their answer to the discovery question, "What's the most important thing to you about the build process?" This is where they told you what they were concerned about and what they were going to be basing their decision on. If communication was most important to them, you say, "And what about communication? Is that still a factor in your decision?"

Now, since we all have a subconscious need to remain consistent with our previous actions, they're going to say "Yes."

"So would it make sense for us to go through both of the quotes together, to make sure that you're getting the best possible price, and also that the communication you need has been factored in?" Of course, adjust the phrasing based on whatever they've said was the most important. If it's the quality of the inclusions, then you could say, "Let's go through the quotes together and make sure you're getting the best possible price and the level of inclusions that you really wanted for your dream home," or whatever it is that matters most to them. You're going to be referencing whatever they told you.

And when they say "Yes," lock in the next meeting with a date and a time. Because we know there aren't thousands of dollars in difference in the cost to build these homes. It's all in the standard that they're built to. If you sit down and explain that to the consumer, you put yourself in pole position. And most of the time, like our research at the beginning of this book demonstrated, you do not need to have the lowest price to win the job.

Objection #5: So and so quoted me x. If you can match the price, I'll go with you.

The way to respond to a situation like that is to say, "Gareth, I'm not saying I can match this price, but if I can, and with all things being equal, why would you go with me rather than (name of other builder)?" Make sure to mention the other builder by name.

Now, this is a key question because the answer they give you will reveal what they like about your building company. "I trust you and your quote was more detailed. Your start date is earlier," and so on. They're going to give you all these things, which will give you leverage to position the value in your price. You're not going to drop it. You're going to position your value.

OUR FIVE-STEP PROCESS FOR DEALING WITH OBJECTIONS

Obviously, you're going to receive other objections as well. It's important to have a framework that you can use to deal with any objection that you find yourself facing. A simple framework to follow is a five-step process that we use ourselves.

Step 1: Let them talk it out.

Never go straight into answering the objection, or even into empathizing. First, let your prospect get it all out. Let them talk and talk and talk as much as they need to. While they do, listen intently. Do not interrupt. That is absolutely crucial.

A lot of people struggle with this because they want to jump in straight away with a solution. But remember that, invariably, the first thing someone says is not a real objection anyway. So, you've got to let them talk in order to get down to the real nitty gritty as to why they don't want to move forward.

Step 2: Empathize and relate.

Once the person is completely finished, then it is time to empathize and relate. "Look, I completely understand how you feel. Some of my best clients also felt that way at this stage of the process."

Step 3: Isolate the objection and frame it up.

Next, you've got to make sure you're dealing with the real objection here. Once they've finished talking, you're going to make sure that there's nothing else holding them back. Keep asking them, "Is there anything else?" until they don't have anything additional to add.

Then you can frame it up. "If we were able to solve that objection, and I'm not saying I can, but if I could, would you be in a position to move forward?" And that's going to allow you to identify if there is anything else potentially holding them back.

Step 4: Answer the objection, then stop talking.

Once you've identified the real objection, you've got to overcome it. And one of the biggest mistakes builders make when they answer objections is that they don't confirm their answers. The problem with that is that they actually end up talking themselves past the close and even end up introducing new objections! This can happen to anyone. So, if possible, use a scripted response to confirm an answer once you've isolated the objection.

This will take a bit of practice because obviously you can't stand in front of people with a script. But first, make sure that you have fully answered the objection by asking them, "Does that answer your question? Does that make sense? Is everything clear now?" Ideally, they're going to make a positive affirmation. "Yes, it does. Thank you." Then, you stop talking.

Step 5: Ask for the action.

This might seem obvious. But again, it's one of the most common mistakes we see with residential home builders in the sales process. They invest all their energy into bringing the prospect to the point in the sales process where the prospect has to take an action, and they simply let the opportunity slip through their fingers.

When the prospect confirms that you've fully answered their objection, you then say, "Would it make sense for us to … ?"

And when they say "Yes," this time, it is now your *Mastercard moment*. Close them on the spot. Never let them go away to think about it. "Okay, do you prefer Visa or Mastercard?"

THE NEXT PERSON TO SPEAK LOSES

Getting back to the standoff between Ryan the builder and Gareth the client, what Gareth didn't realize was that Ryan had an ace up his sleeve. For the previous five days, he had been preparing for this very moment with his business coach. But what Ryan didn't know was that Gareth had already decided to sign the contract; he was simply curious about how this little local builder was going to close him.

But after seven excruciating minutes of silence, Gareth couldn't hold out any longer. He leaned forward, picked up the pen, and signed the contract. And as soon as he did that, they both had a good laugh together because they both knew exactly what had just happened.

The strategy that Gareth was using on Ryan was *the next person to speak loses* tactic. Because in most sales situations, the salesperson will actually talk past the sale and end up inadvertently introducing new objections for the buyer to consider, giving the buyer more ammunition to negotiate the price down.

This happens a lot more frequently than you may realize. And you've probably even done it yourself in the past, out of nerves, the fear of the silence, or because you were being out-negotiated by your potential client. And because custom home builders are often dealing with very successful businesspeople who negotiate deals for a living, the odds are stacked against you. However, when you go into these meetings prepared, and you know what to do, you can hold your own in a negotiation, regardless of who you are up against.

The reason we're sharing this story with you isn't so that you can go out and become a hard-nosed negotiator who intimidates their clients. It's to make you aware that these successful types will likely negotiate right through until the very end of the process. It's also to encourage you to get comfortable with silence. And that could be on a discovery call, where a long pause will encourage the prospect to really open up on a particular thread. It could be when you present a concept agreement to a qualified opportunity and then ask them if they would prefer to pay by Mastercard or Visa. Or even when you get to that final stage in the sales process and the only thing left for the client to do is sign the building contract.

Now that you have some strategies you can use for overcoming objections, in the next chapter we'll cover planning and measuring your key performance indicators (KPIs). In the meantime, you can prepare for advancing your sales by going to www.apbbuilders.com/pbsbook and downloading our cheat sheet for the seven most common objections builders get from prospects.

PART 3:

MARGINS

CHAPTER 7:

PLANNING AND KPIS

It must be borne in mind that the tragedy of life doesn't lie in not reaching your goal. The tragedy lies in having no goals to reach.

— BENJAMIN E. MAYS

One of the most important things for any business is planning and measuring your key numbers. You wouldn't attempt to start construction on a house without detailed plans, and definitely not without doing a take-off of those plans and getting the specific amount of materials that you're going to need. It's exactly the same with your business. It's important to have a clear plan of where you're heading and then to measure your numbers as you progress through the project.

In this chapter, we'll talk more about a few important components that you need to include in your strategic plan. They include the following:

- A SWOT analysis. This is where you analyze your strengths, weaknesses, opportunities, and threats. It's a critically important exercise to complete every ninety days in a building company.

- A BHAG, or a Big, Hairy, Audacious Goal. This is a big target for the future that you're striving towards. It could be ten or even twenty years down the track. Japanese companies actually create a five-hundred-year plan. So, what we're doing here is quite small by comparison, but it's very important to look beyond the next twelve months and even the next couple of years. It's important to create a big-picture vision of your building company.

- A DAD (delete, automate, or delegate), or stop-doing list. The things we need to stop doing either need to be deleted, automated, or delegated. The DAD process is important because every time we add something to our plate, something else needs to drop off.

- Key performance indicators (KPIs) that you will use to monitor and measure your performance.

RUSS'S LIFE LESSON IN PLANNING

Back in 1988, I was living in England and running my first business. I thought I was doing pretty well. And my bright red Porsche parked out the front showed everyone just how successful I was. But the reality was that the business required a ton of cash. I had to hold a lot of stock in my business and give payment terms to my customers. And what that meant was that to grow the business, I had to leave all of the net profits in the company. Meanwhile all my friends were employed by large companies, so they got to spend everything they earned.

I was in my twenties, and I wanted to buy apartments and flashy cars and live the high life, just like my friends. So, I did what any owner of a small business did at the time. I ran an overdraft so that I could pull the net profit out of the business and spend it on investments like a pension scheme, an apartment, and of course, a nice, shiny red Porsche. The bank manager would even take me out to lunch just to tell me what a great businessman I was. I cringe when I think back on this now.

But that all changed in the summer of that year, when a new bank manager took over my local branch of the HSBC in South London. This new manager wasn't so impressed with my business acumen. I can clearly remember the day he came to see me in my warehouse and asked to see the financials for the company. I printed out the profit and loss report and the balance sheet for him. I had no idea what he was looking at, but I was pretty impressed with myself because I was able to print out exactly what he'd asked for.

In my mind, I was a computer genius because I was using accounting software, and I was confident that this bank manager would be just as impressed with my business as was his predecessor. However, when he scrutinized the balance sheet report, he didn't see a successful company. What he saw was £15,000 of net equity supporting a business with annual revenues in excess of £1.5 million. The entire business was being propped up by the bank's overdraft. And they could pull that facility any time they wanted.

He placed the balance sheet on my desk, took off his glasses, and let out a disapproving sigh. "We're not here to fund your lifestyle, Russ," he said quite sternly. I was shocked to hear that. After all, I was the customer here! And a good one at that because I paid interest, I paid bank fees, and I had £150,000 worth of physical stock sitting in my warehouse. I was successful, or so I thought.

But the bank manager from the HSBC quickly brought me down to earth. "I don't like what I'm seeing here. We are providing a £150,000 overdraft on £15,000 equity. The bank is very exposed." Then he said, "What do you think will happen when interest rates go up?" I just shrugged my shoulders because interest rates were already at 10 percent. They surely couldn't go up too much more.

The new manager then announced that, moving forward, he would only be offering a facility that equaled 50 percent of the retained equity in the company. That was 50 percent of £15,000, or £7,500. In one meeting, he was going to reduce my overdraft by 95 percent, take away my working capital, and effectively close down my business! And he could do that because he was the one in control. He was the one funding my business. And by continually ripping the profits out of the business year after year and then relying on the bank to finance it, I'd given them complete control of my future.

What followed that conversation was a little bit of backtracking and a lot of begging, to which he agreed to give me a sporting chance to save my business. What he wanted to see was a detailed twelve-month financial plan followed by monthly in-person meetings where I was to provide the latest balance sheet and profit and loss reports.

In addition, he was going to take a fixed and floating charge over all my stock and also any debtors, which meant he would be following all of the numbers that I produced each month very, very closely. I knew he was serious, and that at any moment he could simply pull the pin and effectively end my business overnight.

Therefore, I had to learn about accounting really quickly, so I immediately went out and bought two books, *Accounting for Non-Accountants* and *Accounts Demystified*. I read all about double-entry bookkeeping, creditors and debtors, assets and liabilities, and even sales cycles. It was absolutely fascinating! And once I knew what my bank manager was talking about, I went to work and produced a detailed plan for the year ahead. I included sales revenue, cost of sales, and every single fixed expense in a detailed budget report. I had one shot to make things right, and no room for error. Which meant the breaking news regarding interest rates was the last thing I needed to hear.

PLAN FOR THE FUTURE (SWOT AND BHAG)

To succeed in business, you must plan out your future and monitor your KPIs diligently. And any plan for the future must be based on actual results from the past, taking into account industry benchmarks to keep everything realistic. You can't simply pluck numbers out of the air or apply your *best guess*.

To do this, you must have up-to-date and accurate financial reports for the last twelve months. For a residential building company, it's best to look at the numbers by quarter rather than monthly. That's because in this industry, the sales cycle is very long, and the number of building contracts signed can fluctuate a lot for building companies below $10 million in annual revenue. Looking at quarterly numbers will give you a better understanding of how your company is performing compared to industry standards.

When you're planning, you must perform the SWOT analysis we mentioned at the start of the chapter. This analysis will identify the strengths of the business, the weaknesses of the business, the opportunities that lie ahead, and the external threats that may be out of your control. Make sure that you involve all the key stakeholders of the company in a SWOT analysis and don't attempt to try and do this on your own. It's always a good practice to involve people who play an important role in the business, such as your management team, because other stakeholders may be aware of opportunities and threats that you do not know about.

Next, get very clear on the fundamentals for your business by determining your BHAG. Why do you want to grow your business? It can sound exciting to double your revenue, but the gloss soon wears off on those numbers when you find yourself working harder and longer while lacking a true purpose. So, it's very,

very important to understand why you want to grow your building company. What's the bigger picture here? What is it that you are trying to achieve?

Now, once you've completed your SWOT analysis and identified your BHAG, next you will need to create your financial plan.

MOVE THE NEEDLE
(THREE YEARS, ONE YEAR, QUARTERLY)

Start with a plan of what the business will look like in three years in terms of the KPIs. What will your revenue be? How much gross profit will you be generating? What will your fixed expenses be up to? And how much net profit will you be generating? Once you've got your three-year plan, you can easily break that down into your one-year plan. Your one-year plan is going to put you on the path to achieve your three-year plan.

Now it's important to remember that growth is not linear. It has an S-curve effect. So, when you create a one-year plan, it isn't simply going to be one third of your three-year plan. If you've got some big growth plans for year three, you're not going to get a third of the way to those growth plans in the first year. There'll be a little bit of a lag before it gathers pace with the growth really starting to kick in towards the end of year two, and then compounding through year three. Bear that in mind when extrapolating your plan.

Once you have your plan for the next three years, break the first year into twelve months for your financial accounting, and then break it into four quarters for your actual quarterly reporting. The quarters are the most important for measuring your performance because you cannot make big strategic decisions for a residential building company based on monthly figures.

Once you've documented your quarterly KPIs, identify the rocks, or the big tasks that you need to achieve in order to hit the numbers in that quarterly plan. You're looking for the big projects that are going to really move the needle. However, never assign yourself more than three big projects, and never more than five for the company as a whole.

Next, look at these rocks, and break up each project into forty-five-minute tasks. Then allocate weekly blocks of time in your calendar to work on these tasks. We call these *sprints*. This is how you will focus on high-leverage work that will really move the needle and propel you towards your one-year goal, which takes you closer to your three-year goal, and ultimately your BHAG.

Make sure that you have enough sprints allocated in your calendar to complete the tasks that make up your rocks within the first twelve weeks of the quarter. Take into account any holidays or time off that you might have planned. It's always best to budget in more time than you think you'll need, or you'll find yourself at the end of the quarter suddenly rushing to complete your rocks. Allocate time to work on your business consistently throughout the quarter.

When you follow this process, you can use week thirteen of the quarter to plan properly for the following quarter. And if time becomes a problem and you simply don't have enough availability to allocate the required number of sprints on your calendar, then you really need to look at your stop-doing list. Look at all the activities that you're currently doing. What can be removed from your plate, systemized, or handed over to someone else?

Use the DAD formula to free up your time. For everything you're currently doing, ask yourself, *Does this even need to be done?* It's amazing how much stuff we do out of habit and just keep carrying forward over the years. But do we really need to be doing it anymore? Does anyone? If the answer is no, then delete it. Simply get rid of it.

There's other stuff we do that with a little bit of effort can be automated. Be careful not to spend too much time automating tasks that don't take up enough time to warrant the time and energy it takes to automate them. However, when you do automate a task, you've saved that time forever. Not just your time, but you're not having to pay someone else for their time either.

So first you delete, then you look at what can be automated. And if it can't be deleted or automated, then you have to look at delegating. Everything can be delegated. Don't fall into the trap of thinking that no one can do it as well as you, or that no one else can even do it. You just need to keep the most important tasks for yourself, the most leveraged tasks that are going to really move the needle. And even if someone else can't do another task as efficiently as you, well, 80 percent is good enough. But when you attract the right team, you'll actually find people who can do a lot of this stuff better than you can.

KEY PERFORMANCE INDICATORS

Finally, we need to establish the KPIs that will drive your building company forward. These are typically broken into two groups: lead indicators and lag indicators. It's important to have a combination of both in order to have a really good understanding of where your building company stands at any one time.

Put these KPIs somewhere prominent so that you see them daily and they remain top of mind. But don't overdo it with numbers. Anything from seven to twelve indicators should be enough to drive your building company forward. Update the numbers weekly for your lead indicators, and monthly for your lag indicators. And then watch those ratios closely and dig into any problems early, especially with the lead indicators where you'll need to make adjustments to your marketing and sales.

LEAD INDICATORS

The first lead indicator that we recommend monitoring very closely is your advertising spend. That's a cumulative ad spend as you progress through the quarter, updating it weekly. You'll also be looking at the number of leads that you're generating from your ad spend. And once you have your ad spend and your leads, you can then calculate the cost per lead (CPL) which you can monitor as well.

Like we covered in Chapter 4, the more information you get about a lead, the more qualified the lead becomes. If you have the phone number of a lead who is looking to build, that is called a marketing qualified lead (MQL). So, you can record the number of MQLs you're getting to determine the cost per MQL. And when a lead has been passed over to sales and has answered the qualifying and discovery questions to your satisfaction, they become a sales qualified lead (SQL), which is when you will schedule a meeting with them. The number of meetings completed is another important KPI to monitor.

The next step in the typical sales process for a custom home building company is to move the prospect into a concept design agreement. You'll want to measure the number of concept design agreements that you sign, as well as preliminary building agreements. Monitor those numbers, as well as the average contract value, and the gross markup that you're applying to each of the contracts that you're signing. A sure-fire way to grow your margins is to record what your margin is every time you sign a building contract. And finally, record the total dollar value for each contract. When you measure these lead indicators, you'll be able to identify the weakest part of your funnel and focus on improving that part first.

LAG INDICATORS

You should measure lag indicators monthly. And the reason for that is they wouldn't make any sense if you measured them weekly since you can only do the work-in-progress calculation for a building company at the end of each month. Lag indicators include sales revenue and gross profit, which is the profit that's actually being realized on your projects as opposed to the gross profit you hoped for when you signed the contract. Also look at your fixed expenses and keep a close eye on those expenses and monitor them as a percentage of revenue, making sure you're below 15 percent unless you happen to be embarking on an aggressive growth strategy for the business.

If you're running a residential building company, you should be striving to meet and then exceed 10 percent net profit. If your building company is making 3 percent or less in net profit, then you have a job rather than a business. You can't scale a building company safely and securely on margins that low. It's simply not possible because as the company grows, your fixed expense ratio will increase, which will eat into your net profit, and you will start losing money very quickly.

You also need to measure your work in progress figure. This is very important for a new home building company because the work in progress accounting adjustment (WIPAA) is the most misunderstood calculation in our industry. Contrary to popular belief, new home builders are actually cash flow positive, which means they are carrying a hidden liability in their accounts. In our experience, most accountants do not understand how to calculate WIPAA correctly for a building company. So, make sure you download the step-by-step guide in the resources section of this book in order to make sure your building company does not become the latest victim. Once you have calculated your WIPAA liability, compare that figure to your bank balance. Your cash and debtors must always exceed your WIPAA and your creditors; otherwise, your company will eventually run out of cash.

Another key number is workflow, although this is a little bit of an intermediary number rather than a genuine lag indicator. Workflow is the uninvoiced amount in contracts you have on your books. It is an indication of short-term cash flow because it is guaranteed income. This figure is often confused with the WIPAA calculation even though it's very, very different. When a lot of builders and accountants talk about work in progress, what they're actually referring to is their workflow. And that's a very different calculation to work in progress, which is an accounting adjustment that goes into your month-end accounts to correct your profit and loss and balance sheet.

And finally, the other lag indicator to monitor on a monthly basis is equity. This is the amount of retained profit inside your building company. In its simplest form, equity is all of your assets less all of your liabilities. It is the total net profit that your building company has accumulated over the years, that you've never withdrawn as dividends. Businesses are structured in different ways, so you might not have any equity sitting on your balance sheet if your building company was set up as a trust. In that instance you most likely have a separate company set up by your accountant for protection. Either way, you need to build up the equity or your *reserves* because that is where the strength of a company lies. And that is what will see you through the next downturn or recession.

To get maximum value from your KPIs, you need to be looking at up-to-date figures. In terms of your lead indicators, looking at live information is crucial. So, when you use software tools like HubSpot CRM, you can build your own live dashboards, enabling you to see exactly how many leads are being generated, how many of those are marketing qualified, how many are sales qualified, how many meetings have taken place this quarter, as well as how many design agreements have been sold, preliminary and full building contracts signed, and so on. All of this information can appear in a live dashboard, so you always know exactly what your conversion rates are.

HOW RUSS NAILED THE NUMBERS

So, back in 1988, I had lost control of my own business. I was now effectively reporting to a manager each month and giving him a full report on what was going on inside my company. And I absolutely loved it! This is because it gave me a level of accountability that I'd never experienced before. And when interest rates shot up from 10 percent to over 17 percent in just a few months, I can honestly say that the reason my business survived was thanks to my new manager at the HSBC.

At the end of the twelve-month reporting period, I delivered on exactly what I'd predicted in my financial budgets in terms of revenue and retained net profit. And in return, the overdraft was set at £100,000 rather than the £7,500 he originally wanted to reduce it to. That was due to what he called "A significant reduction in risk to the bank." However, he did expect the equity in the business to continue growing over the next twelve months and the overdraft to continue to reduce, which I wanted as well since I wasn't too keen on paying 17 percent interest any longer. But it was the forecast expenses versus actual expenses that got me really excited.

I remember sending the manager a fax because that was how we emailed or sent SMS messages back in the day. I asked him, "Did you see how close I got to the forecast?" My actual numbers were within 0.1 of a percentage point. I thought it was absolutely amazing that a number I had forecast a year earlier had been well and truly nailed. I thought that now he'd finally be impressed with my business skills. But all he said was, "Yes, I did."

In all honesty, I never liked that bank manager as much as the previous one who used to take me out to Chinese restaurants for lunch and tell me how great I was. But he has probably been the most influential person in my business career. He has helped to shape the way I do business planning, right to this very day.

So, now that you know the basics of putting together a financial plan and the types of indicators to include and track, you can go to the resource section at www.apbbuilders.com/pbsbook and download our ninety-day planning template. Then, in the next chapter, we'll invite you to reconsider how you are pricing your jobs.

CHAPTER 8:

HOW TO PRICE YOUR JOBS

Turnover is vanity;
profit is sanity.

— UNKNOWN

One of the biggest challenges we see residential home builders face is how to price their jobs. They're unsure how much markup to add to the cost of sales, and ask themselves things like:

- Should I add a dollar figure, or should I add a percentage to the cost of sales?

- Should I try to undercut my competitors so I can win the job?

- Should I be pricing in line with what the client wants to pay (i.e., the budget the client has given you to have the best chance of winning the job)?

But all of those pricing methods will lead to serious problems down the track. Instead, the model that we recommend residential home builders use is what we call *Pricing 4 Profit*. Following the Pricing 4 Profit methodology requires you to focus on your net profit per job, rather than the gross profit. But before we get on to that, you first need to understand the difference between markup and margin. These terms are used interchangeably in our industry and get confused even by some very smart people. However, it is important to realize that these terms are very, very different.

MARKUP VERSUS MARGIN AND NET PROFIT

- Markup is the profit as a percentage of the cost of sales (i.e., your materials and labor).

- Margin is the profit as a percentage of the selling price.

For example, if your material and labor costs are $800,000 for a project and you add a 25 percent markup, that's $200,000. Meaning $800,000 plus $200,000 gives you a $1 million building contract.

However, the margin on this job is only 20 percent, which we work out by calculating $200,000 as a percentage of $1 million (e.g., $200,000 divided by $1 million). Therefore, a 25 percent markup equals a 20 percent margin.

Unfortunately, too many builders mistake their margin for their markup, and because they're not marking up as much as they should be, they are achieving smaller and smaller margins. The problem gets worse. In the example we just used, the builder may be thinking that they have a 25 percent margin because they added 25 percent to their cost of sales (a markup). So, when they look at their accounts a few months later, and they see a $200,000 invoice paid by the client, they do a quick mental calculation: *25 percent of $200,000 means I've made $50,000 profit.*

But since the margin was really only 20 percent, it's $40,000 in profit. That's a $10,000 difference, which is massive when you're working on tiny margins like this. And it only gets worse when that invisible $10,000 profit gets spent. Multiply that with several jobs running at once, and things get out of hand very, very quickly.

What's more, basing your pricing on a markup, or by simply adding a percentage to the cost of sale, can be a dangerous game to play. Because in order to do it successfully, you need to have a good understanding of your fixed expenses and how they apply to each and every job. Fixed expenses are everything it costs to run your business each year from rent and payroll to marketing and advertising (i.e., all of your costs except for materials and labor). When a building company is growing, expenses grow disproportionately to the revenue.

And when a builder focuses more on their gross profit, they typically neglect the net profit and end up simply working for the equivalent of a basic wage. When you work for wages and have no retained net profit, you have a job, not a business.

To grow a residential building company safely and securely, you must price your jobs with the net profit in mind. To do that, you need to add a net markup to your jobs rather than a gross markup on materials and labor. When you add a gross markup, you are simply hoping it will cover all your fixed expenses with enough left over to grow your building company.

You may have heard builders say that although they've grown their business to fifteen homes each year, they were making more money when they were just doing two to three projects. It's because they are using the wrong pricing model! Typically, these guys get burnt out and they scale back down to doing just a few homes a year, and they make more money again. Sometimes they even adopt the mindset that growing a building company is simply growing your problems, so it's much better to stay small.

However, the only way to create a real business that doesn't depend on you is to scale it up. And to do that you need the right pricing model. As an example, refer to Builder A versus Builder B in *Figure 8.1* on the next page. When comparing Builder A and Builder B, you'll notice that in year one, both Builders A and B are doing the same number of jobs: four homes a year. They've got the exact same average contract value, the same fixed expenses, and the same annual revenue. Their net profit is also the same.

Builder A - Step #1 Forecast The Year
(Traditional Pricing Model - Marking Up On Cost)

Financials	YR1	YR2	YR3
Marketing Budget	$5,000	$10,000	$15,000
# Jobs	4	8	12
Average Contract Value	$450,018	$450,018	$450,018
Annual Turnover	$1,800,072	$3,600,144	$5,400,216
Annual Fixed Expenses (inc Your Wages & Marketing)	$200,000	$440,000	$720,000
Cost Per Job Per Day	$357	$393	$429
Gross Margin	13.04%	13.04%	13.04%

Job Cost - Step #2 Calculate The Job Costs			
Materials & Labour	$391,320	$391,320	$391,320
# Weeks	28	28	28
Fixed Expenses	$50,000	$55,000	$60,000
True Cost Of Sale	$441,320	$446,320	$451,320
Markup On Cost Of Sales	15%	15%	15%

Contract Price	$450,018	$450,018	$450,018
Net Profit (Contract Price-(Job Cost+Fixed Expenses))	$8,698	$3,698	-$1,302

Growing The Company			
Retained Profit	$34,792	$29,584	-$15,624
Net Margin	1.93%	0.82%	-0.29%

Builder B - Step #1 Forecast The Year
(New Pricing Model - Setting A Net Margin)

Financials	YR1	YR2	YR3
Marketing Budget	$5,000	$10,000	$15,000
# Jobs	4	8	12
Average Contract Value	$450,146	$461,641	$472,406
Annual Turnover	$1,800,586	$3,693,127	$5,668,874
Annual Fixed Expenses (inc Your Wages & Marketing)	$200,000	$455,000	$755,000
Cost Per Job Per Day	$357	$406	$449
Gross Margin	13.87%	15.23%	17.16%

Job Cost - Step #2 Calculate The Job Costs			
Materials & Labour	$391,320	$391,320	$391,320
# Weeks	28	28	28
Fixed Expenses	$50,000	$56,875	$62,917
True Cost Of Sale	$441,320	$448,195	$454,237
Markup on True Cost (Min 10%, Recommended)	2%	3%	4%

Contract Price	$450,146	$461,641	$472,406
Net Profit (Contract Price-(Job Cost+Fixed Expenses))	$8,826	$13,446	$18,169

Growing The Company			
Retained Profit	$35,306	$107,567	$218,034
Net Margin	1.96%	2.91%	3.85%

Figure 8.1: Builder A vs Builder B

88

However, Builders A and B are using different pricing models. As they both grow from four to eight homes in year two, and then from eight to twelve homes in year three, you'll see that Builder A continues with the traditional pricing model of adding a markup to his cost of sale. That's a dangerous method for a growing building company, and we'll explain why at the end of this chapter.

Most builders add a gross markup to their jobs, but it's not enough to simply make a profit on the cost of your materials and labor. That profit must also be big enough to cover your drawings at a market salary, and all of your fixed expenses. On top of that, you still need enough profit left over to build up your company reserves and fund the future growth of your building company. Remember, growth is not linear; therefore, you need strong reserves.

Overall, a building company that is profitable when it's under $3 million in revenue simply can't remain profitable as it scales beyond $4 million, $5 million, and $6 million unless it uses the right pricing model. If you aren't calculating margins correctly, you will simply scale your building company up to a point where it loses a lot of money quickly.

GETTING CLEAR ON TERMINOLOGY

To price your jobs correctly, you must start by getting clear on the terminology that needs to be used and the industry benchmarks you need to be hitting.

- Revenue = The total amount of income coming into your building company.

- Cost of Sales = The cost for all the materials and labor relating to construction. It's any cost that can be directly applied to a job.

- Fixed Expense = Any company expense that cannot be directly attributed to a job. Payroll for off-site employees, rent, marketing, advertising, virtual staff, and software all appear in your fixed expenses.

For example, the invoice you get from the concreter can be applied to a specific project; therefore, it is a cost of sale. However, your estimator's salary can't be attributed directly to an individual job. It can be spread across a number of jobs, but it can't be applied to an individual job; therefore, that is considered a fixed expense.

Also included in your fixed expenses are the owner's drawings. Your drawings must reflect a market salary for your position (i.e., how much it would cost to hire someone to do your job). If you follow poor advice of not drawing a salary and simply *fixing it up* at the end of the year, you end up undervaluing yourself and under-pricing your jobs. You must pay yourself first in business.

If your business is in the early stages and you simply can't afford to pay yourself a market salary from the start, then that's fine. We all have to make sacrifices to get things started, but your goal should be to raise your owner's drawings to a market salary as quickly as possible to avoid under-pricing your jobs.

But make sure you don't overpay yourself either. If your company's making good money, then you can draw additional payments as shareholder dividends. Running a building company is like having two jobs. The first job is working in the building company as the director, and the other role is the shareholder (i.e., the financer). Keep these roles completely separate. And in the role of a shareholder, you should expect a return on investment. It's no different than if you put that money in the stock market or bought an investment property.

Refresh yourself on the differences between markup and margin:

- Markup = Amount of profit as a percentage of your cost of sales.

- Margin = Amount of profit as a percentage of the selling price.

- When it comes to profit, there is gross profit and net profit.

- Gross Profit = (Revenue - Cost of Sales)

- Net Profit = (Revenue - [Cost of Sales + Fixed Expenses])

If you're not currently including your owner drawings in the fixed expenses and you are simply drawing out all the profit the company makes at the end of the year, then your company has zero net profit and therefore zero percent net margin. Your company has little value because it is not profitable. All you're doing is creating a job for yourself and not a profitable, scalable business.

To better understand how your building company compares against the industry benchmarks for gross profit, net profit, fixed expenses and more, download our free video training by heading to www.apbbuilders.com/pbsbook.

So now that you understand the terminology and the benchmarks, it's time to create a plan for pricing your jobs.

THE PLAN

By now, you have a clear understanding of where your numbers are and have completed your one-year plan, as we covered in the previous chapter. And once you have a clear idea of the number of jobs that you're planning to do over the coming twelve months and what your fixed expenses are, you can start pricing your jobs correctly.

To do this, you need to understand the fixed expenses for each job. And to do that, you need to know how long a typical job included in your plan from Chapter 7 is going to run. First, establish the number of weeks it takes to complete a project of that size. Then, multiply the number of weeks the job is going to run for by the number of jobs that you intend to run for that year So, if your average job runs for 26 weeks, with contingencies, and you plan on doing twelve jobs over the course of the year, that is 312 weeks.

You then divide that figure by the number of working weeks in the year. So, if you shut down your offices over Christmas for 4 weeks, for instance, that leaves you with 48 working weeks in the year. Maybe you only shut down for 2 weeks at Christmas and then another 2 weeks over Easter. Either way, you need to remove those weeks of downtime because there won't be income coming into the business.

That leaves you with 48 working weeks in the year. Divide 312 by 48, and that gives you 6.5. This is the number of concurrent jobs you will be running at any one time. Slightly more than six jobs, in real terms. Now you know that if you can only run six jobs maximum at any one time, then you're going to either have to build a little bit quicker or you are simply not going to complete twelve jobs in the year.

Now, look at your fixed expenses again and make sure those fixed expenses will cover the number of concurrent jobs that you are now planning to run. Do you have enough resources in place? Do you have the software you need in place? Do you have enough staff and supervisors to manage that number of concurrent jobs?

Once you're satisfied that your fixed expenses will allow you to run those jobs concurrently, the next thing to do is calculate the true cost of sale for each job. To do that, look at your fixed expenses for the year. For instance, if that was $360,000, divide that figure by the number of working weeks in the year. If that number was 48 weeks, then that figure becomes $7,500 per week. So, you know that your business is costing you $7,500 a week just to operate. If you divide that figure by the number of jobs running at any one time, or 6.5 in our example, that means each job is costing $1,154 a week to run.

To go a step further, if you divide that figure by five, you get a daily rate. Based on our example, each job costs $231 a day in fixed expenses, just to run. So bear that in mind whenever a consumer asks for a variation that's going to add another two days onto the job. In order to cover your costs properly, not only do you need to add on what that variation is going to cost you in materials and labor, you also need to add on $462 to cover the cost of the delay (e.g., two days using the daily rate of $231) and the impact that is going to have on your ability to build the number of homes that you're planning to build to be at full capacity.

If you don't add this cost per day onto the variation, it will come out of your pocket at the end of the year in the form of a reduced net profit. With every delay, keep this in mind. Your project manager should always know this figure, and every time a subcontractor doesn't turn up onsite, this is the true cost to the business of the ensuing delay.

Each job you price is going to run for a different amount of time. There are going to be very few jobs that actually hit your average contract value or average schedule timeline. So, whenever you price a job it's very important that you also schedule it out at a reasonably detailed level. For example, if you take on a larger job that's going to run for 36 weeks, then multiply $1,154 (the weekly cost of running the business in our example) by 36. That gives us $41,544. Now that figure needs to be added to your cost of sale, or the quotes that you've received from subcontractors and suppliers.

If you've been quoted $500,000 by your suppliers and subcontractors, you now need to add $41,544 to that job. This gives you a true cost, otherwise known as your breakeven figure, of $541,544. And whatever you add to that figure becomes net profit.

To achieve 10 percent net profit, you will need to add an 11.1 percent markup. Adding 11.1 percent to $541,544 gives you a contract price of $601,655.

THE SECRET TO BUILDER B'S SUCCESS

Circling back to our example of Builder A and Builder B, Builder A continued to simply add a markup to their cost of sales, while Builder B committed to the

Pricing 4 Profit model. Over the coming years, they both grew their building companies at the same rate. However, because Builder A continued with the traditional pricing model, even though their annual revenue was over $5.4 million, they were losing money in year three. And because Builder B worked on the Pricing 4 Profit model, they continued to increase their margins to ensure they were making a retained net profit.

And although Builder B was nowhere near the industry benchmark of 10 percent net profit by year three, they were able to grow their building company reasonably quickly and make some profit while doing so. The real difference here is that Builder B was making $218,000 net profit, even while having higher fixed expenses than Builder A, whereas Builder A lost money.

Remember that expenses grow disproportionately quicker in a building company. Typically, what happens is that builders start out working on very low margins when quoting jobs because they have very low overheads. This then forms a pricing habit. They mistakenly believe, "If I had more revenue, I'd have more profit, and then I'd be able to afford to pay more staff, and so on." But a building company just doesn't scale in that way.

Instead, you've got to work on bigger margins from the beginning, even though you can operate on smaller ones. If you don't, you will never scale up your building company successfully. You'll forever be working on low margins for undesirable clients. You might only win jobs because you're the ridiculously cheap option—and you won't be able to afford to advertise or market your company. And that means you'll never be able to generate more demand for your services and you'll forever be stuck on the hamster wheel. However, if you price your jobs with margins that hit the minimum industry benchmarks, you'll be able to grow your building company safely and securely.

Your building company has got to be making adequate net profit simply to ride the S-curve. Growth is not linear. You take a small step back in order to take a huge leap forward. If you're already losing money like Builder A, growing and adding more revenue compounds your problem. If you're thinking, *I just need more sales. I need to go from $5 million to $7 million, and then I'll be all right,* you will lose even more money. The fundamental problem for Builder A was their gross margin, not their revenue.

Now, to relate this to an actual person, when Rick Champlin from Simple Group in Utah approached the Association of Professional Builders looking for help with his building company, one of the first things he did was the Pricing 4 Profit training. After that training, Rick went on to make sure that they accounted for all their overhead whenever they priced a job, and that's something that they weren't doing at all previously. He now considers that training to be one of the most valuable.

Rick's company also started using the Pricing 4 Profit calculator that is included in the Pricing 4 Profit coaching course in conjunction with our KPI ninety-day planning spreadsheet that we mentioned in the previous chapter. This helped them understand what their overhead numbers currently were, what they were likely to be in the future, and how much needed to be added to jobs that were going to run for different lengths of time to make sure that they always cleared an acceptable net profit on every job.

Now you should be clear on the differences between margin and markup, gross and net profit, and why these distinctions matter. In the next chapter, we'll explain how to create demand for your company so you can schedule your jobs more effectively for the next twelve months and beyond. In the meantime, head to www.apbbuilders.com/pbsbook to download video training on the industry benchmarks for gross margin, net margin, fixed expenses and more. You can also download our detailed guide covering how to price your jobs.

CHAPTER 9:

DEMAND AND SUPPLY

Strategy without tactics is the slowest route to victory. Tactics without strategy is the noise before defeat.

— SUN TZU

It's very important for residential home builders to focus on demand and supply in order to put themselves in a position where they are always booked out. It sounds simple, but it's so important that builders have the mindset of generating more potential clients than they need or are able to service.

The goal must be to generate twice as many preliminary building agreements as contracts because that will put you in a strong position. Most builders aim to close 80, 90, or even 100 percent of PBAs that they sign. They wear that as a badge of honor. "Everyone who signs a PBA with me goes to contract." But that is a bad situation for a building company to be in.

Ideally, you should only be progressing 50 percent of your PBAs into building contracts to avoid becoming too reliant on your clients at the PBA stage. When you get used to closing 80 percent or more of your PBAs, your cash flow and your profitability will be adversely affected whenever a client fails to progress into a building contract due to unforeseen circumstances, which puts you in a very vulnerable negotiating position with your remaining clients at the PBA stage. So, by deliberately engineering a situation where you have more PBAs than you can take on as building contracts, you actually change the balance of power between you and your potential clients. You are the builder in demand, which makes your building company a scarce resource that can charge a premium for its services.

However, creating more demand in the sales process than you can supply is only half of the story. The other half of the story is creating a balanced funnel all the way through the build process. Otherwise, you end up in a situation where you have a lot of jobs starting at the same time, which means you will experience a shortage of trades at different points in the build. What's worse is that you will not have the time or the resources available to deliver a world-class handover experience, which for the client is the most memorable part of the whole experience.

SUCCESS WITH CONSTRUCTION SLOTS

When Rocky Simmons from Vision Homes in West Virginia walked into his lawyer's office to drop off a new agreement, it was just as the U.S. presidential elections were taking place in November 2020. He and the lawyer had a bit of idle chit-chat about the election and how the result might affect business. The lawyer said to Rocky, "Tell me, how many jobs do you price that never ever get built?" Rocky smiled and said, "Well, prior to July of 2019, a lot. But now, we only price for the people who actually want our help." The lawyer was a bit bemused by that response and said, "Well, what happened in July 2019?" And Rocky said, "That was when we started using construction slots."

That date was also when Rocky became a private client of APB, which is how he discovered construction slots. In this chapter, we'll explain how construction slots can also help you increase demand for your building company.

WHY DEMAND AND SUPPLY IS KEY

The key formula that leads to success in business is demand and supply. And as business owners, we all know this to be true. However, we tend to forget it because we're too close to the action. For builders, this is even more important because the sales cycle is so long and the number of sales that a builder makes in a year is really quite low compared to other businesses. And if you are supplying all your demand and then two or three PBAs drop out of your sales funnel, it has a devastating effect on the profitability of your business for the next six to nine months.

There is no way to predict what might happen to a consumer's personal finances and all the ways they might find themselves in a situation where they can no longer proceed with building their dream home. There are a lot of things that can change, so if you're relying on a large percentage, like 80 percent or more, of those PBAs progressing to contract, your building company and your livelihood are in a very vulnerable position.

Most residential building companies increase their supply, which is their resources, in line with the demand for their services, right from the moment they start out. They get one job, then two, then three, and so on. And when they take on more projects, they increase their resources to service that growth. The problem is that when the demand drops off, builders have to chase more jobs in order to feed the beast that they've created because they now have so many additional fixed overheads in place. And when they chase work, the first thing that they compromise to win that work is their margin.

The goal for a residential building company is to always be booked out. In which case you will need to have more demand for your services than you can satisfy at every step in the sales process. This creates desire because we all want scarce resources. As soon as something becomes abundant, or even just available, it's suddenly less appealing.

A waiting list means that you will ultimately be turning clients away. You have to get comfortable with the idea that some people won't wait for you to build for them. They're going to go elsewhere. When you embark on this strategy, it's very important that you do not buckle when clients try to pressure you into increasing your supply. If you increase your availability on the fly to meet demand, that will not only undermine your strategy, but it will also undermine your integrity. Everything has to be planned in advance and adhered to.

PLANNING TO BE BOOKED OUT

To start your planning, refer to the business plan that you've created in Chapter 7. Look at the number of jobs that you're planning to start in the next twelve months. Then, stagger the start dates for those jobs over the course of twelve months. Another thing to keep in mind, particularly if you have projects running for different lengths of time, is the target handover dates for each of these jobs. It's a good idea to ensure that they do not finish at exactly the same time either so that you aren't handing over several jobs at once. So stagger your start and finish dates using the construction slots methodology. You now have your available construction slots, along with the start dates.

These slots can only ever be allocated to a consumer once a project has building approval and the deposit has been paid. Never allow a consumer to book one of your available slots without both of these requirements being satisfied; otherwise, you will lose all of your leverage. A slot can only be allocated once all factors out of your control have been dealt with and the project is ready for construction to start.

The reason it's important to have a limited supply in relation to demand is to avoid ending up in a situation where you spend nine months working with a consumer to design their home, get all the engineering done, the specifications nailed and spend weeks pricing it—and then just as they're about to sign the contract, the husband says, "Well, I've just spoken to another builder and they'll do it for $x." Or "It's a bit over what we originally spoke about nine months ago and we can only afford to pay $x." Whatever the reason, some people will attempt to renegotiate before they sign on the dotted line.

As a builder, you can find yourself in a vulnerable position where you're banking on that contract starting in the next few weeks to inject some much-needed cash flow into your building company. But when you use construction slots, and you have two PBAs for every available slot, you genuinely don't mind if a customer wants to think about it. That's fine! You've got another PBA who will take that construction slot. And the people who need to think about it will just have to put their name down for the following slot once they've made up their mind. That's not being pushy or salesy, that's being a professional service provider. You offered them first refusal; the decision is theirs.

Slot availability can always be spoken about in the sales process to make prospects aware that this is how your company operates. You can also go on to explain that it's why you can guarantee the construction start date when your competitors can't. But you cannot allocate a slot at this early stage; otherwise, you will undermine your whole strategy, which is to create genuine scarcity and urgency. They are the two things that you need in sales in order to be successful.

But using scarcity and urgency is a dangerous game if you don't do it right, because the moment you buckle, all your credibility is lost. The key is to keep it simple.

KEEPING IT SIMPLE

When you embark on this strategy, keep things as simple as possible. So, once you have your construction slots in place, keep aiming for at least two PBAs to be ready in time to fill each one. Even if you're in a comfortable position at the moment where you're signing up 80 to 100 percent of all your PBAs you should still be aiming to generate more PBAs. What we often find when we analyze a building company that typically signs 80, 90, 100 percent of their PBAs is that they are marking up their jobs below the industry benchmark of 33.3 percent on new homes (25 percent margin) and 50 percent on renovations (33.3 percent margin).

The idea is that you're not going to simply cut down the number of houses you build because you've only got x number of PBAs. The goal is to double the PBAs to give you more options. So, you will have to build up your advertising, your marketing and your sales strategies to double the PBAs that you're currently generating.

The goal is to be able to sign two PBAs for every contract you need. Once you have that, you will have genuine scarcity and urgency. Then, you can look forward to being booked out and creating a queue of clients for your building company. This is how you build out a solid, predictable workflow at margins that exceed the industry benchmark.

A WIN-WIN POSITION

Once Rocky discovered construction slots in July 2019, he started staggering his start dates and planning out his year in advance. And what that allows him to do is space out his trades, which means he's never short on labor now. And the handovers are evenly spaced out as well which makes it a lot less stressful for the administrative team in the office.

In Rocky's own words, he said that when he started implementing this, "It was fantastic because for new prospects, I was able to show how much demand there was for our services, which built trust and allowed me to create urgency for people to take the next step and get moving on the design."

Rocky also said that it has been great for him and the construction team to be able to plan what they have coming up and take some time to see what areas might be vulnerable. Because of this, they are able to spot potential bottlenecks way before they happen. As of November 2020, Rocky was already booked out for the first nine months of 2021. This is exactly what the APB told him would happen when he first embarked on this strategy back in July 2019.

What that means is that Rocky and Vision Homes are now in a position to make good choices. The decision Rocky was looking to make in December 2020 was whether he should increase his capacity for 2021 or continue booking out his construction slots into 2022. To help him with this, he was able to simply plug the numbers into his APB KPI spreadsheet to create a *what-if?* scenario and see if the extra work was going to transition to real net profit that could get added to the bottom line. If not, he could choose to stick with building twenty-five homes for the year and instead focus on increasing his margins and filling up the construction slots for 2022. He found it absolutely incredible that in November 2020, he was already talking about construction start dates as far ahead as 2022.

Not only do construction slots help with getting consumers over the line, but they also help with your strategy to increase your margins overall. When you've got more demand than supply, then you can experiment with increasing your pricing. As new people come into the design process, you can start setting those price expectations higher. Because you are booked out, you are the builder in demand! You are the builder everyone wants to build with, and your prices should reflect that.

In the conclusion, we'll wrap everything up with some next steps about APB coaching. In the meantime, you can go to the book resources online at www.apbbuilders.com/pbsbook and download a copy of our Construction Slots Template to start planning out your next year.

CONCLUSION

The main thing that we hope you take away from this book is the belief that there is an easier way. Too many custom home builders are stuck on the hamster wheel, doing the same thing they've always done, because they believe that's just the way it is. They think they have to provide free quotes to consumers, who will then choose the lowest price, which means the builder will never be able to earn a decent margin on the work they do.

Instead, we hope that you will take inspiration from all the examples of builders who have implemented these strategies and not only changed their businesses, but really changed their lives as well. We want you to see that there is a better way of doing things. You don't have to carry on working for wages.

Because when a building company fails, we've seen firsthand the devastation that causes. Builders have to sign personal guarantees with suppliers, so when their business fails, they lose everything: their livelihood, their home, their marriage. It destroys lives. And one of the main causes of this is that builders simply don't understand how to look at their financials. They don't realize the danger their company is in until it's too late.

When we are able to show builders what's on the horizon, what's coming up in a year, even eighteen months' time, and then help them to change direction—it's like they were flying in a plane that was heading toward a mountain and we helped them to alter their course. When you know you've been able to save someone from that kind of devastation, it's incredibly rewarding.

We also get immense satisfaction from working with builders who were doing okay, but then went on to the next level. These are builders who were operating in the mindset of, "There's no point in making more money. You just pay more tax." They now admit how ridiculous that sounds. But at the time, we had to guide them out of that mindset, then provide them with the systems to earn a significant amount of money—we've seen a lot of our members go from an income of $100,000 a year to over $500,000 a year in less than three years. The reward is getting to see how that then changes their lives. Now they're taking their whole family on overseas trips. They're building nicer homes for themselves, with swimming pools. They're buying nice cars. They're living the life that a professional builder should be living, rather than the life that the average builder in this industry lives.

START WITH THE FUNDAMENTALS

When you start implementing what you've learned in this book, it's important to start with the fundamentals. Otherwise, you're just going to end up spinning your wheels. It's really important to do the right things in the right order.

Start with the fundamentals that we covered in Chapter 1. Get really clear on who your ideal client is. Then, start building your brand around the things that your company stands for.

Once you've got those fundamentals in place, you then need content to attract your ideal clients into your world.

Once you have a process that works for attracting ideal clients, then it's time to scale that process through paid advertising. We see a lot of builders make the mistake of thinking, *Now's the time to grow!* And that they just need to put an ad out and they'll get more clients. Unfortunately, it just doesn't work like that. You must follow a proven process that can be scaled up through paid advertising. Just throwing money at advertising on its own simply won't cut it.

Once you do start advertising, you're going to find yourself with a lot of new leads. This can be a problem if you don't know how to separate the wheat from the chaff. Chasing all of them will lead to poor-quality opportunities that will consume the majority of your time without producing any revenue for you. It's important to follow the qualifying process that we discussed in Chapter 4 to focus on those prospects that are most likely to proceed into a building contract at a decent margin.

To maximize the opportunities in your marketing and sales funnel, you must follow up on every qualified opportunity. And when you do follow up on those quality opportunities, you must always be advancing the sale. Those are two key skills that you really have to learn to be successful in any business. Learn how to overcome objections and close the sale because nothing happens until something is sold. Don't avoid that challenge just because it makes you feel uncomfortable.

When you've systemized your building company, the pace of growth will come very, very fast. This means you must know your numbers which means monitoring your KPI dashboards daily. You've also got to have a flight plan of where you're heading. Stay focused on the bottom line, or the retained net profit (i.e., after all expenses and owner's drawings have been taken out). That's the bit left over to support the business growth. If you do that in a custom home building company, then the cash will look after itself because building new homes is cash flow positive!

If you aren't calculating your work in progress figure each month, then you will find yourself in a situation where cash flow is masking your losses and you simply don't realize that you're losing money. Use the Pricing 4 Profit strategy in this book's resources to make sure that you are always adding a net profit onto your jobs.

And then, to increase your margins, use the law of demand and supply that we discussed in Chapter 9. That will help you with both growing your building company safely and securely and also growing your margins.

MINDSET

To execute all of those things, you have to have the right mindset. Brian Tracy speaks in great detail about how each of us has a self-concept of how much we think we're worth. He says, "We have a mental block inside us that stops us from earning more than we think we are worth. If we want to earn more in reality, we have to upgrade our self-concept." He states that none of us are able to earn 10 percent more than our mental self-concept, or 10 percent less.

If we find ourselves earning 10 percent less than our self-concept, we end up engaging in what's called *scrambling behaviors,* where we go all out trying to make up for the shortfall. We work longer, harder, and we find opportunities, until we bring our income level up to a level that we truly believe we're worth. It's exactly the opposite when we find ourselves earning too much. We've seen people earning more than they believe they're worth start engaging in what's known as *compensating behaviors.* They find ways to sabotage what they're doing and effectively get rid of the money so that their income comes down to a level that they're comfortable with.

So, it's very important to understand that to earn more, you have to raise your self-concept. That can't be done in one fell swoop. You can't go from being worth $100,000 a year in your mind to $1 million just like that. Your subconscious simply won't accept that. You have to do it gradually. But this is why it's very important to work on your mindset.

A FIXED VERSUS GROWTH MINDSET

All the strategies and tactics in this book will not work for everyone. There is a famous scene in the film *The Matrix* where Morpheus says to Neo that they never attempt to free a mind beyond a certain age. It's too dangerous. It's exactly the same with us at the Association of Professional Builders. We never attempt to enlighten a builder over the age of fifty-five because those builders are generally too set in their ways. They have spent too long doing things the hard way and can't face the fact that they've spent the last thirty to thirty-five years of their life working for a wage when they could have made some serious money. To accept this as being true would be an admission that they've wasted thirty to thirty-five years of their life. Instead, they get angry. They argue, and they deny that it is possible.

This is why, if you speak to an older builder, they'll pooh-pooh a lot the strategies and tactics being used by our members as being something that wouldn't work for them or wouldn't work in their area. They simply can't accept that there is an easier and better way of doing things.

And that's the difference between a fixed mindset and a growth mindset. A fixed mindset is where you believe that the skills you've been dealt in life are fixed and cannot be improved. With a growth mindset, you believe that all skills are learnable and that you can achieve anything with the right knowledge and the right application.

It's very important to move forward with a growth mindset when you're executing these strategies and tactics. The younger builders in their twenties move incredibly quickly through the strategies outlined in this book because they have no mental blockages. They have no preconceived ideas or doubts in their mind. They just execute, and as a consequence, they get results quickly.

Older builders in their forties are still open-minded enough to try things, but they're a little more cautious, a little more doubtful. They move slower. And as a result, the results they get are slower as well. They do get results, but not as fast as the younger guys who are all in from the start.

APB COACHING

If you carry on doing what you've always been doing, you're going to get what you've always been getting. To grow your business, you need to learn new skills. If you are a custom home builder and you have a desire to grow your building company, both in terms of revenue and in terms of profitability, then you need to join the Association of Professional Builders.

We've lost count of how many builders have told us, "My building company wouldn't exist if it wasn't for the Association of Professional Builders." We hear this over and over again, often from people who appeared to be doing well when they first came to us. They might say something like, "I'm not doing too badly, but I'd like to improve a bit." Then, after a couple of years of working with us, they're so grateful. They say, "I didn't realize just how bad things were at the time. My company wouldn't be here today without you guys and what we've been able to implement."

And for builders who are looking for personal mentoring and coaching, we offer the opportunity to some of our members to become private clients and work with an executive coach in the APB Mentoring Program. One reason that the APB Mentoring Program is so successful is that we don't follow the traditional consulting model. That model is similar to going to a surgeon and telling them you've got tonsillitis, so the surgeon removes the tonsils without any further diagnosis. They just go by what the patient tells them.

What makes the APB Mentoring Program different is that we use a process called Data-Driven Decisions (DDD) when we work with builders. This means that we listen to what the builder is telling us about the challenges they're facing in their business, but we make sure to also look at the data before we prescribe the solution. We can do this because we know all the industry benchmarks and the KPIs of all our private clients, which enables us to identify the real problem in any individual building company, rather than their perceived problem.

If you'd like to join the Association of Professional Builders and be a part of this movement to improve the construction industry for both builders and consumers, then head over to our website www.apbbuilders.com and take a look inside. And if you haven't yet downloaded the free resources mentioned at the end of each chapter, make sure that you go to www.apbbuilders.com/pbsbook to do that as well.

Printed in Great Britain
by Amazon